PEOPLE

To Aswin,

People are a pain
in the neck, or are they?

PEOPLE
Managing Them (and Yourself) Effectively

Richard Smith

Published by Levelplain

This book is presented solely for educational and entertainment purposes. The author and publisher are not offering it as legal or other professional services advice. While best efforts have been used in preparing this book, neither the author nor the publisher shall be held liable or responsible to any person or entity with respect to any loss or incidental or consequential damages caused, or alleged to have been caused, directly or indirectly, by the information contained herein. Every company is different and the advice and strategies contained herein may not be suitable for your situation.

Dedication

My inspiration to write this book was Mary to whom I have been married for nearly a quarter of a century. This book took me close to seven years to complete which was two years longer than Mary took to write and publish 6 books including one that hit the New York Times bestseller list. Wow, I could feel pathetic if I was not me. Mary helped me with every aspect of this book, for that and for her very existence I am eternally grateful and I look forward to the next quarter century.

To my daughters Ciara and Cliona who like their mother, never stop amazing me, I love you deeply and nearly equally.

Contents

Introduction

Welcome.

I expect nearly all the people reading this book work for an organization of some sort. It may be a privately-owned business, a national not-for-profit charity, a medium- or large-sized corporation, or some other entity. Whatever the structure of the organization, there are many different realities its employees, managers, and leaders have to live with and not all are easily understood or obvious.

It takes a lot of effort and thought to understand the true meaning of situations, or the behavior that is expected of you when some ethical test presents itself. You may struggle to make the right choice, or misunderstand someone's true intent and respond in the wrong way. You have to find ways to work through any and all challenges and find, maybe not the perfect solutions, but at least livable solutions. You already know from experience that the more you practice at something, the better you will become.

There must be a point to what you do for a living, or it leaves an unsatisfied gap in your life. I am not talking about the meaning of life. (Besides, everyone who has a sense of humor knows the answer to that is 42.) I'm talking about not living life with the false expectation that your job alone will make your life worth living. That sort of value is not what you should expect from your work life. Recognize and accept that work is simply work; in the majority of cases it's what you do, not who you are. Your work may be a vocation or just a way of making money to pay for the things you need and want. So, if you must work, then find some ways to enjoy it or to at least get through the day with a sense of achievement. If that is not possible, then try to find a way to have the odd laugh or reason to smile.

For the last two decades, a large part of my work day has been spent managing — people, projects, time, and expectations, among other things — and that activity called "management" is what I am interested in dissecting and describing. In this book, I will touch on many aspects of what I call "Managing While Being a Human." It could be described as an obscure art, and one that is rarely discussed in business schools and even more rarely practiced in the workplace. Much of what you read in these pages may surprise you and, ideally, make you (re)think about what passes for the norm in corporate culture. Some of what I say might even be considered subversive, but I maintain that both individual managers and entire companies can thrive by following the guidance in this book.

Reading this book with a beer, a glass of wine, or a good Scotch in hand may enhance the experience.

People

Part I – People

People

Chapter 1: Heroes are Not Welcome

I have often heard praise for people who went above and beyond what was expected of them, who saved our bacon, who made that super-human effort. Almost universally, organizations celebrate that level of effort and encourage it. Many people will follow that lead and do what is encouraged and what will be rewarded.

But, you need to ask yourself if this extra effort is what a company or its customers need. You must ask if it is sustainable, reliable, or safe. Is it *really* better to be a superhero than to be a steady, simple, boring manager? I think it is not. If there is less drama in the workplace, there is less make-believe. Less fantasy.

Take a step back from the "heroic manager" scenario and consider the following question: Is it best for the company to plan the next project, the next commitment, the next strategy, based on the idea that collecting a few overachieving "heroes" together, giving them capes, and asking them to wear external underwear and fight the good fight will bring better results than pulling together the regular team of regular folk and simply asking them for team work, commitment, and follow-through? I do not think the hero approach makes sense and, too frequently, it virtually guarantees you a whopper of a disappointment. Superheroes, by definition, need big problems to solve or they lose their membership in the club. If you ask around, how many companies do you think would prefer continually dealing with big problems requiring dramatic solutions over enjoying a calm, steady, dare I say mundane existence? I doubt the answer would surprise you.

I've worked in several industries and in many different roles, and my experience has shown me that the world is full of good, normal people who are happy to work hard to achieve something in which they have even, perhaps only, a modicum of interest. These people do not need to be treated as if they can fly unaided, with only their magic underwear for support, or as if they can bore holes in a safe with their eyes from across the room. For corporate management to believe that employees must be treated as such borders on condescension, and it doesn't go over well in the break-room. What employees want and need is to know that the task they are being asked to do is reasonably achievable and that, if they express their opinion, it will be listened to and taken into account. Not necessarily acted upon, just taken into account.

Scenario 1

Sara was called into the divisional head office to be given her next program assignment. Business was going well, very well indeed, and now the company needed another production line opened in its South Carolina plant—yesterday. Sara knew her stuff and was well respected. She formed a team, made a detailed plan, and effectively managed the program. There were numerous and enormous challenges and many changes as the program ran, but the team led by Sara took it all in stride and delivered. Sara succeeded through detailed, realistic, but aggressive planning. The team rarely saw her flustered and everyone had their heads down from start to finish. The CEO got to know Sara's name and was extremely happy not to have been needed to reset the project at any stage or get more involved than necessary—freeing him to concentrate on other business needs.

Scenario 2

Fred never had the plan straight on paper when he launched the new software development effort and, six months in, things began to unravel. The division head and the CFO called many meetings, which they neither wanted to be a part of nor had the time to be a part of. Over the course of two scary weeks they worked with Fred, helping him to gather his thoughts and guiding him while he formed a new plan. After this hard reset, and with dedicated effort from the expanded team, the software package was delivered six months late and over budget, but just barely in time for the show at which the CEO was to present the new product. In the hero culture, Fred is held up as a great example of what perseverance can achieve because he "saved the day"; he gets rewarded and publicly praised. The fact that he had let the program go off the rails is conveniently forgotten because now he is the hero. His "heroic" effort saved the CFO and division head from embarrassment, so they were happy to deploy some short-term memory magic and hold Fred up high as a hero for saving the project (and them). Fred's team, however, didn't forget that his project meetings had all been very tense, rife with constant reminders of the importance of the project and the need for super-human efforts on their part, all while working under a consistent state of severe pressure — thanks to Fred. His team did not appreciate the high praise for Fred when they'd had to experience the pain of the process.

For long term success, you need more people like Sara and fewer people like Fred.

You can still achieve great things even when the capes remain in the closets. You just need to drop the reliance on heroes and instead ask for hard workers, and then steer them toward their goals and reward their achievements.

Every project and every situation will have its own set of challenges, but if whatever it is that you are trying to achieve is carried out in a calm way, instead of with fuss and drama, then you and your team deserve high praise and the rewards that go with it.

Chapter 2: Be Yourself! Always. Everywhere.

When this book is reviewed, I expect that critics will say that it seems like a bit of philosophy and a bit of business and a bit too much of a rant, and that it doesn't have enough of a how-to focus. I talk about work, happiness, behavior — but what is the *focus*? I can hear them asking. Why don't I stick to work or to home life? Why blend them?

Well, the philosophy that I subscribe to is that you need to be consistent in your behavior whether you're at work or somewhere else. I know that you deal with a lot of situations at work that may never happen in your personal life. For instance, you never have to consider mass layoffs at home. Nor do you need to be careful whether you leave the seat up at work. I am talking about the approach you take when facing a situation. I know many people who say they behave like a different person at work than at home. I've heard many different reasons and rationalizations for it, too. "I need to be tough at work." "I do not trust people in the office." "My boss expects me to be a suck-up."

Here's my advice: Do not act differently at work than you do at home, and vice versa. Do not attempt to be someone you are not. It's too much effort and it doesn't work, anyway. If you are an asshole at home, I doubt you will be able to hide it at work, which means that very few people will want to work for you, and you will not get the best from them, if they do.

You do, of course, need to control yourself and use good judgment when expressing your opinions, but you still need to be yourself. Being yourself instead of being someone you think you should be allows you to lose the baggage of trying to keep up an act or trying to track what bull you said to which people or which group. It's difficult to keep track of lies; it's much easier on your brain, your conscience, and your stress level to be honest. Consider: If you're always honest and occasionally forget why you made such and such decisions, then you can construct the reasoning from first principles every time and will not have to worry about what lies you manufactured along the way. This removes a significant pressure from your life.

I realize that right now you're probably thinking, "I just want to shout at everyone to grow up or to stop being lazy, but I can't really be myself or be honest about that."

Wrong.

For one thing, that sort of "being yourself" is not wh
about. It's not the thought that's wrong in that example, it'
The shouting method is a great example of boorish, ill-mannered, altogether too-common behavior. Aside from what that approach says about you to upper management, it doesn't deliver ideal results. What I'm saying is that you can communicate the same sentiment in a more civilized way with the happy result that you will get the message across in a way that will effect positive change. Behaving like the mature adult and good manager that you are will also release some of the pressure inspired by the minority of people you need to engage with on a daily basis who are immature, lazy, or just incredibly annoying.

Be genuine, be yourself. It makes life so much easier than does the alternative.

People

Chapter 3: Help, I Need Somebody! (The Great Standoff)

You must help people. It's what a good boss does; it's what a bad boss does not. Letting people founder in a mess, whether they've created it or not, does not help any situation—ever. But managers do it all the time, calling it "tough love" or "the consequences" or some other term they've made up to dodge the responsibility of doing their job. No matter what you call such behavior, it's unhelpful at best and ultimately destructive to your own goals.

And it leads to the unhappy reality that it just plain sucks to work for you.

I sometimes think of this jerk-like behavior as similar to a situation in which bystanders ignore or fail to help an obviously distressed person. I can think of only a few reasons why a person would do that — and none of them are flattering. They include laziness, mean-spiritedness, cowardice, and fear.

When on the tube in London one day, I came onto a platform and was waiting for the next train. While I waited, a man came along and joined me on the platform. I was watching him and saw that he half-stumbled. I am embarrassed to say that I thought that I should ask him if he was ok, but I hesitated. He was probably 65 years old and a relatively frail version of that, so the first thought that came into my head was that he may be having a heart attack, but again I hesitated. I am sure you have been in similar circumstances at some time. So, there I am thinking that this man may need some help, but I am stuck. It took a few more seconds, but I did manage to shake myself out of my stupor. I went over and asked him if I could help. It turns out he had walked a bit too fast from his last train and was feeling slightly dizzy, but otherwise was ok. I stood there with him for a few more minutes and then went on my way at least having offered helped and happy that he was back to normal. You need to help others in life and in work. After a bit of practice, you will find it gets easier and that people respond by helping you in return.

Consider this: would making "you must help each other" a requirement for your group or team improve the environment and/or the performance of your company? I'd hazard a guess that some of your problems happen because there are people in your organization — maybe even *you* — who just do not see helping others as an appropriate

12

solution, particularly when they (you) can sit on the sidelines and just be righteous without being called on it. Am I right? Be honest (see Chapter 2). I'm guessing you are normally far from perfect yourself. So, stop calling people idiots; stop saying they made their messes and have to clean them up alone. *Help them.*

To be clear, I am not advocating doing people's jobs for them and I am not telling you to "help people help themselves" because I think that's a bunch of childish, patronizing psycho-babble. But if you are not actually helping *your* people, then you are hindering the entire operation. That's not what you get paid for, and it's not what you got promoted into management for.

One oft-repeated argument against helping people out of a mess is that it will be seen as accepting, if not encouraging, bad behavior. And they'll take advantage of it and keep screwing up, knowing you'll bail them out. Well, I am sure some people will *try*, but you are not blind to that possibility and, therefore, you can take care of those people. The fact that you *might* get taken advantage of does not mean the practice of helping others is wrong. Granted, helping your people is not the only thing that you need to do to be successful. But it feels right and sounds right and experience supports the premise that it is the right thing to do.

You *must* help people. When it comes to managing people, nothing is simple or one dimensional. There are a lot of aspects to consider when you're trying to motivate people or make headway on a project. I can assure you that sitting on the sidelines and pointing out their mistakes is not going to fix any problem. Ever.

People

Chapter 4: People are Awkward

Here I go starting off a chapter with a negative statement. However, the title works and states precisely what I want to say; but let me add that awkwardness is not necessarily a bad thing.

When you have the responsibility of managing people, you need to understand how they think and how they react to events and situations. One thing that you can absolutely count on is that on any, if not every, given business day, situations will arise that will be awkward and will involve people. For instance, someone will take offense when you say something that, to you, seemed innocent. People will worry about things that *you* know are non-issues, but you forgot to tell them were non-issues. Some people will misinterpret nearly everything you say to them or that they read, hear, or overhear.

Just like death and taxes, situations such as these are inevitabilities; try as you may, you can't avoid them. So, learn to go with the flow and deal with these situations in a competent, cool, and understanding way. And never forget that this applies to people at all levels. Your personal response to identical situations may depend on whom you're addressing; some people will require one sort of response; others will need the same information delivered in a completely different way. As a manager, it is part of your job to think about *and understand why* different people will react to your message and to anticipate *how* they will react. It is not easy to get it right all the time or even most of the time, and you will be surprised time and time again.

If your solution to negating people's awkwardness is to see yourself as a team of one, and your plan requires everyone to do what you tell them to do and not to question you, your grand scheme will fall to pieces in short order. Why? No one will be acting out of respect for you or your leadership, and they will only do what they have to until the day they are so looking forward to arrives: the day you get your comeuppance.

In comparison, think of a situation in which five or six people in your immediate family or a close social group–a group that appears to be composed of like-minded people, or at least people bonded together in some way—have reacted to the same set of circumstances very differently. Maybe it was that big dinner event at which all six of you were present, when Joe did not appear until one hour after everyone was expecting him. Who got angry that they had to wait for dinner? Who just soaked it in and had another beer? Who was angry, but said nothing?

16

Who jumped down Joe's throat before he could even explain his tardiness?

Managers and leaders need to have already learned the basics of human behavior, if they expect to be effective managing people in different situations and circumstances. It will be to your benefit to spend time stepping back, watching people's reactions, and accounting for them. You do not need to condone or put up with bad behavior from anyone, but you should not be surprised when there is a wide range of responses to one situation. It is okay to introduce emotion into the mix here. People are emotional beings; not squishy emotional, but all have emotions and to understand people you need to account for their state of mind.

Check any thesaurus: 'awkward' has many subtle variations to it, each of which you can match to people you manage and the situations they encounter. For instance, 'uncooperative,' 'embarrassed,' 'inept,' 'obstinate,' 'out of your depth,' and 'clumsy,' are all synonyms for it. How many of those words could you associate with people you know? If you consider the variations on the theme of awkwardness and how you would handle the responses they describe, you can better prepare yourself for understanding, managing, and leading people.

People

Chapter 5: Education is King (Or Queen)

When I refer to education, I do not mean only formal education. I mean both the act of learning or the result of formal education, which is knowledge. Maybe a better title for this chapter is 'Learning is King (or Queen)', because it is through education that you learn and, thus, know things, and through learning that you improve yourself and your understanding of everything around you.

There are many ways to educate yourself and none is more simple, important, or satisfying than reading. People need to read. People need to read for work and to read for pleasure. There has been so much information put to paper by experts and idiots alike, on every conceivable subject, that it will take a concerted effort to find the information you need in a form that suits you. But, the effort expended in the search is worthwhile and, if you do not actively seek knowledge, then you will be missing out on the opportunity to learn. In some respects, it doesn't matter what you read—from methods and best practices for raising hens in your backyard to how to spot a sociopath in your midst. You will learn something new and it will be helpful or applicable in unanticipated ways, from solving a problem at work to making small talk at the company Christmas party.

That being said, don't go mad and sign up for a class or purchase a book that doesn't interest you. Whether you are going to undertake to learn more about a subject you already understand or learn about a new subject, make sure it has a chance of being useful to you. Don't waste your time or intellect.

Likewise, in the workplace, don't waste your employees' time or intellect by making them undergo training that is pointless or of marginal utility just to tick a corporate box or to spend the money in the budget so that you do not lose it next year. I have seen too many cases of people just spending time and money for absolutely no good reason.

If you believe there will be benefits in sharing knowledge, then you must tailor the undertaking to the intended audience. Do not assume one size fits all. For example, a class that addresses the sales process and is specifically tailored to sales people should not be presented to a group of engineers, unless the material is revised to fit the audience. A detailed presentation about leads, pre-sales, and proposals would be email-checking time for the engineers, whereas a general overview of the sales process would be valuable because it would expand their general understanding of organizational operations. But, to really benefit the organization, why not give the engineers training on better ways to use some of their sophisticated design tools to produce higher quality designs in half the time? Provide your team members with subject matter that will benefit them *and* the organization, rather than make them educational tourists merely stopping off at foreign ports on an expensive, but marginally useful cruise.

When considering the effectiveness of education and the learning expected from it, consider the environment in which the education takes place. I highly recommend taking the person or people out of their daily surroundings. Get them away from the continuous email stream and into a place where they can concentrate on the course at hand. Another consideration is how and when the students will be able to apply their new knowledge, because the best results will happen if the students can put what they have learned into practice soon after learning it. This has the obvious benefit of converting your company's training dollars into cost savings or profits more quickly. Should you provide education opportunities to someone just as a reward? Yes. Why not? People like a treat and when a company lavishes some money on them, they feel more valuable. They feel special, and everyone likes to feel special.

'Lavish' may seem like the wrong word — it connotes wastefulness, but in this case, I see no reason *not* to lavish perks on your better people. I have heard it said many times by otherwise intelligent people that if a company provides training to people and through this training they gain new or enhanced skills and knowledge, they could use the new skills to their advantage and make themselves more marketable. Translated, this

21

means the newly educated employees could become a flight risk, going to another company and therefore wasting the money that came out of your budget.

I have one word to say about that: *Really?* Come on! Is your company such a messed-up place that a better-trained person cannot be rewarded appropriately (with a promotion or raise) and made more useful within your company (given more responsibility) thus increasing your profits (bring in more money!) because of their additional training? When you hear stupid statements about the dangers of providing education to employees and about the (imagined) potential disloyalty of people, then it's better to be alert than paranoid. If this is how you or your company sees things, then I guarantee that the company has some bigger cultural problems that need to be dealt with.

There are always things you can learn and areas in which your knowledge and effectiveness can benefit greatly from others, so invest your time and your employees' time in books or more formal education, it will improve the bottom line—guaranteed.

Chapter 6: The Importance of Cheerleading

I was once described as the chief cheerleader at a company where I worked. I do not look much like a Dallas Cowboys' cheerleader, nor do I act out in such exaggerated ways. But the description fits because an important part of what I do inside any company I work for is to encourage and celebrate the team's (company's) moves and plays, successes and efforts. When I am not tossing around my verbal pom-poms, people have also commented that I must have special glasses that have a rose tint to them, implying that I perceive reality in a more positive way than is realistic. I am a realist and see things as they are, both positive and negative, but my 'critics' are right about my positivity. I *choose* to be positive and work through difficult situations with the goal being to find a working solution through hard work and study as soon as possible.

There is a place—a valuable one—for cheerleaders in an organization and I am not in the slightest unhappy with the comparison. After all, in all but the most extreme situations, there will be things under your control that can improve the possible outcomes, if you only think positively.

Things do get tough at many different times of the year—end of the quarters, end of the fiscal year, budget-setting times, the end of big projects—and people will be under many different pressures. When things get tough what should you do? Sit around and moan? Give up and shout out in despair? No matter what the problems that arise, everything will pass at some stage: a solution will be found or the importance will diminish as other things take precedence. So, focus on that—the expected eventual positive outcome—and have *that* drive your thoughts and actions. If you have confidence that everyone who works for you will stand up and put forth their best effort during a time of pressure and crisis, or that you can drive people to stand up, then you have increased your chances of early success ten-fold.

You must also always put things in perspective and ask yourself what will happen if you do not solve the issues completely or at all? What will the real impact be and how bad will it be? Rarely are the consequences a matter of life and death; usually they are a time delay on a project, or a prolonged period of feeling uncomfortable and having little control.

Pom-poms work on a football field but, in-house, people like to see the cheerleader with pizza for obvious reasons. Could it be that people like to be fed something tasty, rather than endure the bitter taste of misery? Instead of relying on a glittering, sequin-covered outfit to change the mood, maybe the situation can be improved with the occasional joke. Instead of jumping up and down like a lunatic to encourage better performance, maybe take some time to recall the last issue that was successfully resolved without loss of life. It would help to improve the situation and get the team on the right track. If none of these suggestions work, you can always find the other cheerleaders on YouTube, I suspect. But give these a try first. That way you won't have to sit through a mandatory training session on Sexual Harassment and the Workplace.

It is crucial to the spirit of any team, group or individual to have a leader who can help show the way in a time of crisis. If you are the right type of leader, then you will not only have the experience, but the natural demeanor to encourage people through thick and thin. You have seen movies in which the coach gives a rah-rah speech that is taken to the extreme. You know the scene I am talking about: There is one minute left in the game. Your team is behind by a single goal. The coach has called a time-out and is surrounded by the players, who are downbeat and all but defeated. Within the very few minutes of the break, the coach recalls their childhood, something about an old dog, and the father they never really knew. The team is inspired — teary-eyed, even — and off they go 'pumped-up' and ready to win. While this film version of rousing the troops is extreme, there is still a place for the rallying cry.

Let me share this somewhat bittersweet story from my own experience. It's a good illustration of how difficult situations can be dealt with to get to a win-win for most people, and how cheerleading can help. I led a great team of developers in a company producing some leading-edge, world-class software. We had only one problem, and it was 1,500 miles away in our corporate headquarters. The problem was not technology, not people, not politics; it was real estate. The company just had too much of it and needed to consolidate locations. We had nine months to make the move, but we also had to deliver our next generation product at the same time. Many in the team chose not to make the move, meaning the team that needed to complete and deliver the product was going to be smaller than we needed it to be. It was a difficult situation, but not uncommon. My role was to ensure that business went on while people were packing boxes and while the countdown was on everyone's mind. This is exactly when the cheerleader in me was needed most. I spent a lot of time talking with the team, being positive but realistic, encouraging them to finish their time with the company on a high by delivering a great product that we would all be proud of. We could have spent all that time moaning and groaning, but that would have gained us nothing. By helping the team concentrate on the positive outcomes and being the cheerleader, we did succeed. Everyone worked at full speed up until the final move day and the team produced a great public safety product that is still in use today, and is saving lives.

Be a good leader and make sure that you stay positive; it is well known that a positive attitude or a negative attitude from a leader is infectious. This means that the response you get from your team will be a reflection of how you present yourself and how you handle situations. In fact, there is a biological explanation for the mechanism of mimicking others' behavior. Check out 'mirror neurons' if you get bored. (See Chapter 5 on reading new things. See, I do follow my own advice.)

People

Chapter 7: "Thinking" is an Action

Use your brain and think.

It's not a radical concept. So why do I even have to remind you to think? After all, you are an adult and it is obvious to you that thinking is required in most situations. Unfortunately, people don't always remember the obvious things in life. You can recall times when you missed something obvious, like overlooking your car keys that are sitting right on the counter because you 'know' that you never leave them on the counter. It's unthinkable that you would have put them there. Or you just didn't think to look for them there, most likely.

You cannot do your best work or attack a problem efficiently unless you have spent real time analyzing the situation, exploring options, thinking through solutions in your head or on paper, and then deciding what there is to do.

People

In his book *Surely You're Joking, Mr. Feynman!* (*Adventures of a Curious Character*), renowned physicist Richard Feynman tells the story of having developed a knack when he was young for fixing the valve-based radios in use at the time. He was asked to help fix a radio that whined badly on startup, but settled down after a few minutes to work correctly. Upon arriving at the radio-owner's home, he was shown the radio and, to the frustration of the owner, just stood there for a few minutes. Eventually, the owner asked when he was going to start working on the problem. Feynman replied that he was working on it; he was thinking about what could be wrong. After pondering possible causes for a little while, he got out his tools, made an adjustment, and solved the problem. The lesson here is that taking action is rarely the best thing to do first—unless you're standing on a sidewalk and a piano is falling toward your head. In that case, trust your built-in reaction system and save the thinking phase for later.

Observing people's reactions to challenges is always interesting. Sometimes, the reactions can be bizarre. For instance, there are people who like to make dramatic statements ("Hark! I come bearing bad news.") only to stop there, presenting their audience with a pregnant pause, during which you are apparently supposed to simply wait for their next statement. But the expected "Gather 'round! Here's the news!" never happens. The pregnant pause lingers. And lingers. Until someone cues the person to keep talking.

What do these people think is meant to happen after their big lead-up to what should be an announcement? Are they lonely? Do they need attention? Were their mouths about to seize up and they felt they had to exercise their jaws? As the manager, it would benefit the group at large to suggest to everyone, including these special snowflakes, that it would be more impressive if they thought through the situation, came up with some thoughts on how to address it, and *then* shared the problem *and the solution* with the whole group.

Another situation in which thinking can come in handy is when something has annoyed you. The temptation is to react swiftly and without enough thought.

Don't do it.

Keep your mouth shut and your fingers off the keyboard, or you will end up compromising yourself, possibly looking a bit foolish, and probably exposing yourself to ridicule or worse.

Instead of reacting to the situation, *respond to it.* Slow down. Think. If needed, think twice. If you are itching to fire off an email, don't put anyone's address in the To line—that way you can't send it out by mistake. Then rewrite that email you want to send. Ask yourself a few more questions to understand the true reasons for your annoyance. Think first. Respond later. Or, perhaps, not at all.

I know that having to think is sometimes a pain in the neck. However, you will, at times, be required to prove that you have actually thought through something and that what you are proposing can be shown to make sense, be possible, or at least be probable. When faced with having to prove that you can support your case, you have some choices: You can decide to be arrogant and refuse to explain yourself. If you are the big boss, maybe you can stomp your feet, declare that you are right, and insist that everyone just get on with the 'doing' now that you have taken care of the 'thinking.' Even if you could get away with it, I do not recommend this approach.

However, you probably aren't the big boss and, therefore, must prove that you have thought through the problem. In this situation, the only real option is to get on with it: share the proof of what you thought and why you came to the conclusions you did. You will win over most people with a demonstration of some facts and some logic.

I contend that many people do not think often enough, or at least are not critical thinkers. Yes, I really just wrote that. Furthermore, I am certain that you can think of too many people and too many situations in your own environment in which behaviors or outcomes were appalling and appeared to be the result of a complete lack of forethought. I have even heard people say, "I don't get paid to think." It's amazing, really, that such a statement would ever be uttered. Granted, there are differing skill and intelligence levels within any group and it does occasionally happen that persons whom you might declare as illogical actually have spent time thinking about the problem at hand. They just happened to come to an odd-ball solution that made no sense or was only partially right. However, such an outcome is likely going to be better than, or at least more adaptable than, one from those who have chosen not to think at all.

People

To think or not to think is a choice people make. As their manager, don't let people get away with *not* thinking more than once. Unless you are managing an army of automatons, thinking is part of everyone's job. It is part of *your* job to convince them of that, so make sure you have not put inadvertent barriers in the way of those who want to contribute the use of their gray matter to the problem at hand.

People

Chapter 8: Listen

It took me a long while to realize how important it is — in work and personal life — to listen. Such an admonition is not psycho-babble. There is always much more to learn than you already know and it turns out other people may have the knowledge that could help you. These people will not get a chance to tell you their ideas or share their knowledge unless you give them a chance to communicate it to you — unless you *listen to them*.

You know how it goes when you are in a discussion with someone and you have strong feelings about the topic. You are sitting at the edge of your seat waiting for your turn to sound intelligent and you are practicing and repeating your 'special and very interesting' point in your head while the other person is talking. Then your chance comes and you blurt out your amazing wisdom. I'd wager that, at least half the times

35

you do that, you miss a substantial piece of the conversation and may even end up repeating something said just moments earlier. The net result is that you don't sound brilliant; you sound like you weren't paying attention. This makes you look inattentive at best and, more probably, rude. This happens even more often in a group. You have only one out of, say, five chances to speak. I advise you not to contribute if you are not paying attention to the conversation. How you could possibly have anything of use to say if you are not actually mentally present and engaged in the conversation? The harsh truth is that you are ignoring four other people while you polish the utterance that you expect will impress everyone. Next time, do the radical and unexpected thing: Shut down your ego and listen for a while!

Another, even more obvious and inappropriate situation in which this happens is in interviews. You know the kind I'm talking about: the kind in which the interviewer does all the talking—and I mean *talking*, not asking questions. The purpose of an interview is to understand and get the know something about a person you have just met and probably know nearly nothing about, or to learn about a situation, project, etc. Too many times, I have seen the interviewer doing all the talking and I've wondered how, exactly, did the interviewer expect to find out what he or she needed to know?

Don't be that person. When you don't listen, you squander what might be your only chance to learn what you need to know. Time will run out, the interview will be over, and you will know no more than you did when you started. In fact, the net result may actually be worse than not having learned what you were supposed to. If you recognize yourself as a person who behaves like this, who talks more than listens, who genuinely likes to hear yourself talk and considers what you have to say fascinating, you may end up reporting that the interview went well and saying that you had a great rapport with the interviewee when, in reality, it went badly and you established no rapport at all. Who looks good now?

So, please learn to listen. It may turn out that no one has anything new or worthwhile to say, but this is rarely the case. If you believe that nothing of value is ever said and that listening is a waste of your time, then you have bigger personal problems than you realize. You need to go and fix them before further exposing the rest of humanity to more of your "brilliance."

People

Chapter 9: The Most Uncommon Sense

Why is 'common sense' so uncommon? Rene Descartes defined common sense as "sound practical judgment derived from experience rather than study." Most of the people in any workplace who have been there for a few years should have a degree of experience. Others will have experience and some amount of more formal knowledge, whether from academic courses, exposure to industry material, or having read books on a subject. Yet, their decisions sometimes still leave you scratching your head. So, what is lacking? Is it that people do not have sound practical judgment? Maybe. But these same people manage to live lives outside of work, juggling many priorities and generally solving and acting on hundreds of day-to-day problems.

I think the lack of common sense can be distilled down to the 'sound' part of Descartes's definition. A lack of common sense in a company executive can have a serious negative effect on the people he or she manages and deals with as a peer, and it needs to be addressed. I believe it's possible to teach people to use a measure of common sense, even if it is your common sense that you train them to emulate.

A simple way to get people thinking sensibly is to ask the question "If you had to handle this situation with your own personal time and money, what would you do?" When presented with this question regarding a situation they faced, in which no common sense has been used, people generally get a bit embarrassed. In many cases, their embarrassment stems from their decision to treat the situation as if it was not worth their effort to resolve it and, frequently, the false hope that someone else would take care of it later. Presuming, as stated earlier, that the person you are questioning has some experience, their failure to use common sense might be because of laziness, passive aggression, some arrogance and, occasionally, revenge. If the person is new to the company or to his or her role, inexperience might be acceptable as an excuse — *once*. But if the person doesn't cop on fairly quickly, that sends its own message to people above, below, and adjacent on the org chart.

Scenario:

After many years of hard work by the sales and pre-sales teams, your company has been invited to the bid on a potentially profitable and very high-profile contract. The company is buzzing. There is only one week to get everything together — the pricing, the service contract details, the terms and conditions. John and Jennifer are taking the lead and will ensure that the proposal goes out on time, is world-class, and will help win the deal. One-hundred-and-twenty pages later, the tome is ready and reviewed and is shipped off ahead of the deadline—but only by a few hours. John and Jennifer follow-up the next morning, as usual, to get their tracking number and send it on to the customer. That's when they realized that this is not going to be a good day for them. It turns out that the team in shipping had learned from the carrier that it would cost a lot of money to send the packet overnight and they were all too aware of the well-known corporate initiative to save costs. So, they decided that for half the price it could get there in two days instead of one.

Even though the packet was marked "urgent," someone in shipping thought about it and came up with the wrong answer to the question "How much of a difference could a day make?" Now, the inclusion of common sense in that thought process would have considered the option of acknowledging the sender's decision to mark it *Urgent* and, therefore, to treat it as such, or to at least tell the sender about the desire to adhere to the cost-savings plan. In the end, after much groveling and persuasion, the customer accepted the submission one day late. The company did not win the bid and maybe it was not related to the shipping issue, but this is a common example of what can happen when common sense is not used.

Be vigilant and do not assume that people have common sense, or that they will use it all the time if they do have it. You must find ways to teach people common-sense responses to situations or find others who have it already. In any organization, you must also be sure that there are

41

no barriers to the use of common sense, such as processes that are too controlled and take away decision-making opportunities from people, or situations in which the leaders in the company do not allow others to contribute.

Chapter 10: The Perfect Boss

There are many people involved in running a business, whether the business is successful or not. So, how do you determine the good from the bad? Let us start by describing the traits perfect bosses possess.

- They filter most of the bull for you.
- They share the glory with you.
- They are readily available, not constantly available.
- They let you decide important things when you are the right person to make the decision.
- They delegate well and make sure the team is fully used as part of any solution.
- They do not sweat the small stuff.
- They preach, practice, and require flexibility.
- They are fair, but can be tough, as needed.
- They make grown-up decisions.
- They help you advance, if you deserve it.

People

Chapter 11: The Prefect Boss

And then there was Billy. It was not worth the effort to work out what was going on in Billy's head, but what was coming out of his mouth and email were easy to work out. He appeared not to like life or himself too much. He was a Neanderthal and why someone had thought it was a good idea to have Billy in charge of humans was bewildering. Perhaps putting Billy in charge was the result of joke day at the office: it was the one of the most ridiculous things they could think up. I call him the Prefect Boss.

The term *prefect* has connotations of spiteful control, if you believe ubiquitous stories of the student-turned-supervisor in British boarding schools. There are several varieties of boss that exist within the Prefect archetype. Look for the traits described here and measure your boss against them to find out if he or she is a Perfect boss or a Prefect boss.

45

The Cling-On Boss: This is the boss who stands over you and cannot leave you alone to do your job. Cling-On bosses think that the only way to get work out of the lazy people — their name for their staff — is to control with an iron fist. When they take a break from micromanaging their underlings, they may make obscure references to cricket or baseball bats.

The Arm's Length Boss: This is the non-clingy version and is no better than the Cling-On. When you need their help, these bosses are never available and do not want to get too closely involved because something may make them look bad. Arm's Length bosses may also be delusional and think they are 'above it all' and, therefore, won't lower themselves to learn about and/or get involved in the details.

The Hands-Off Boss: This boss is careful and devious and will not take responsibility for a decision. He or she will, however, make sure to attribute the more dangerous decisions to you and make *you* go through the process of justifying *his/her* decision, which was made prior to even posing the question to you. This is an especially soul-destroying exercise and one that a Dementor would be proud of. I am sure I saw the Prefect boss type in a supporting role in the *Harry Potter* novels.

The Hard Man Boss: The "Hard Man" prefect boss likes to bully and make examples of people. There should never be a place for this sort of boss in any organization, although they have not yet gone extinct. Let me be blunt: no one should ever end up crying because of treatment at work, and anytime this happens — and it does — I guarantee that something is badly wrong with your organization. Take it upon yourself to figure it out quickly and solve it.

In the workplace as in the schoolroom, all prefects have their favorites and, just like the memory of the popularity contests in school, the end-game may have nothing to do with the institution. More likely, it is about some personal trial the prefect went through at some point. Irrespective of the cause, the result is that people are treated differently, and badly at that. When favoritism is alive and well in the workplace — and try to find one without it — it will kill all good will in that group or department.

The Prefect Boss has many different traits and comes in many versions. If you need a test to determine whether a boss is a good boss or a bad boss, then ask yourself the following question: "If I behaved toward the boss in the same way as she/he behaves toward me, would she/he be okay with that?"

When faced with the prospect or the reality of working for and dealing with a bad boss, keep in mind that it is rarely possible to change people and 'dealing' with the problem boss quickly becomes tiresome. The options before you are to wait for another to come along or to leave and go somewhere else. Neither option is ideal. The third option is to become the boss and see how you would do things differently.

People

Chapter 12: The Perfect Employee

How would you describe the perfect employee? "Perfect" may be setting the goal a bit too high, but let's leave it there for now. You don't actually need perfection, but if someone working for you were to come close, then all the better for them and for you. I will not set about describing a list of astonishing traits of future world leaders or what would be expected from a genius. As discussed earlier, it is neither reasonable nor expected that the perfect employee is a super hero. However, it is completely reasonable to expect that the people you hire will be good people who regularly achieve good things and are capable of doing great things on occasion.

The perfect employee works intelligently, and I am not talking solely about people in high-status jobs. Think about the employee who consistently ensures that the company mail boxes are filled with the correct mail and rarely makes a mistake. This is intelligence. Think of the employee who thought to put two items that were going to the same address into a single package and saved the company from wasting even a few dollars. This is intelligence.

Another simple thing you can expect from perfect employees is that they are reliable and actually show up when they are expected to do so. Showing up at work should be a simple thing to manage, but experience indicates the act is not easy for many people. The perfect employee is dependable.

A perfect employee is flexible, or at least not too rigid. Businesses can be complex entities with a lot of moving parts that can operate differently, depending on the circumstances. Selling to one customer may require much more effort than selling the same product to another. The assumptions you used yesterday to make decisions may need to be changed to something very different today. Both work and life involve dealing with changes, some of which are more slow-moving than others. It's important to be aware of what is changing around you and what the big, small, immediate, and long-term impact of those changes could be or will be.

When you encounter change, you need to be able to react in a flexible manner. There are few things that can ruin my day faster than hearing an employee state that, "We cannot deal with this or that because it is not how we normally do things here, so the customer is just going to have to wait and that is that." A close second is the drama that ensues when someone make a show of getting around the process and expects big congratulations. These are two good examples of what the perfect employee will never do to you or your customers.

Perfect employees get satisfaction, and possibly pleasure, out of the job they do. The fact is that work is called 'work' for a reason, and it is not always easy. Sometimes, it's not much fun, either. Most of the time, what is needed to get work done and achieve your goals is straightforward, but it can sometimes be tedious or unexciting at the same time. Therefore, a company aiming toward success needs to have employees who actually like to work, and who like coming to work. I am not suggesting that employees have to like or enjoy everything they do. You cannot realistically expect that for them or for yourself, but I am suggesting that a company needs employees who accept work as something that can actually be fulfilling and that they can get some pleasure from. Imagine a whole company of these people; I think it would be a successful company and a good one to work for.

A perfect employee gets on with people socially. All work situations require us to deal with situations and people. The company's customers are normally human, or closely approximate humans, and ditto for your work colleagues. Nearly every day, you will encounter and need to deal with people, and if you know how to treat and interact properly with people, then you will be more successful in work. Being a socially aware, thinking person can also lead you to see signs of stress or issues with those around you, allowing you to adjust your manner, if needed.

The perfect employee also has a skill. Did I mention this yet? The perfect employee is useful at something and, if the stars are aligned and the moon is in the right quarter, then her skills match the job you are paying her to do. Of course, having people do the job you want them to do does require you to be very clear about what their job actually is. A job description is a good idea, but do not become a slave to it. Let it evolve, just like humans do. Well, at least as some do.

The perfect employee has a strong sense of self-respect and will not put up with any muck or disrespect, and will not intentionally do anything that is wrong, no matter who asks her to do it. Asking one to do the wrong thing is a good way to get rid of a perfect employee. And possibly your own job.

I am happy to report that, in my time in the business world, I have met a good number of people who clearly match my description of perfect employees.

Chapter 13: The Imperfect Employee

Imperfect employees are willing to give only 50 percent of their effort and expect or contrive to make other people to do the remaining 50 percent of their work. Their behavior becomes obvious to their co-workers, who must complete the work or clean up the mess resulting from an incomplete job. Imperfect employees are adept at rationalizing their behavior. Some of the more popular rationalizations are that they think they are too good to be doing work they see as 'below their station' and that they are not paid enough for such and such a job. For someone who is comfortable with self-delusion, it's not only easy, but satisfying to create myriad "sound" reasons to justify his/her behavior.

I maintain that if employees, myself included, do not want to play fair and give their best to the job, then they ought to go away and find something they find more suitable to their skills and expectations. Under ordinary circumstances, the company is expected to nurture worker productivity through its organizational structure and the availability of the right tools. The worker reciprocates by working hard for an agreed-upon wage.

Consider the effects of a half-assed program manager—I mean imperfect employee—who was the first person in charge of a multi-year project. The pain of cleaning up the messes he created will likely outlast his tenure on the project or even at the company. Imperfect employees often leave a traceable path of frustration and chaos in their wake.

Let me be candid: dealing with imperfect employees is a pain in the arse. There are better uses of your energy than dealing with an employee's bad behavior on a day-to-day basis, so address it head-on. One way to do this is to do yourself and the imperfect employees a favor by helping them on the way to their new career. Let them know unambiguously that you are on to them. Suggest that if they want to put in half the effort, you'd be happy to halve their pay to accommodate that. Present them with the option; maybe there is a job out there for them that will not expect their full effort for a full pay package. They may thank you for giving them the opportunity.

Imperfect employees are often unhappy, bordering on miserable, and unfortunately this can be contagious and affect those who come in contact with these people. For the good of the organization, they need to shape up or ship out. Do not let employees who can destroy a good working environment drag others down to their level.

54

Another trait indigenous to imperfect employees is that they think everyone else is doing a bad job and are more than willing to spend a lot of time pointing this out to others. In addition to being generally shoddy behavior, this displays their ignorance. Every employee, discipline, and department in a company faces unique demands placed upon it, and people outside the situation rarely fully understand what those demands entail. It would be nice if the complainers would make an effort to learn what they are talking about before they start pontificating, but that would undermine their true agenda, which is to distract attention from their own underperforming selves.

Then there are the imperfect employees who play the system. You know who they are. They take extended sick leave for no believable reason, or always seem to use up their sick leave at the very start of every year and miraculously are not sick again all year long. They are more than likely trying to play the game. What can make this situation worse is if they think you know what they're doing and they do it anyway. Besides being arrogant and devious, this defiance undermines your authority and spells trouble.

No business owner or manager should have to tolerate useless people. The biggest and most destructive outcome is not the decrease in that individual's productivity, but the effect on other employees who witness the behavior and silently boil away on the inside because it is not addressed. This situation can inspire stronger negative feelings toward the manager of the troublesome person than toward the troublemaker. This redirection is an interesting phenomenon; unfair, but very human and very common.

Everything in this chapter applies to all levels of an organization and applies just as crucially to those doing manual labor in the company as to the chairman of the board. None of them can be imperfect employees if you want the best from your company. It is important to remind yourself that you cannot change people. But you can determine employees' strengths — even imperfect employees have them — and find a way to put them in positions that utilize those strengths. But if their strengths — complaining, sloughing off, or dropping the ball — are not needed in the organization, then no organization can afford to keep them.

Chapter 14: Teamwork

When people talk about their company and express with pride that the standout performance is because of great teamwork, my first reaction is that this team explanation may not be the real root of their great performance. I find that success is not as often the result of the total effort of the team per se or a team-structured approach, but is the result of great individual skills applied in a successful collaboration. I will explain this subtle difference and why I believe it is important.

Successful companies need to have a collection of individuals who do their jobs well and who apply their specific skills effectively. On top of this, a company needs to organize and allow a loose confederation of these individuals who, when coordinated, achieve expected results. So maybe teamwork is not the right angle, because the environment for success comes from strong, performing individuals led by a strong, performing individual. So, what every organization needs are more individuals who have useful, well developed skills that can be applied to your particular project or challenge, and who can work closely with other individuals who are also skilled and will deliver their part of the puzzle.

Teams will generally be composed of people with a wide mixture of personality types, performance capabilities, and actual levels of performance. Some teams are good, some bad, and some very ugly. (Organizationally speaking, of course. We are all beautiful inside.) But teams are often also hiding places where individuals who are weaker than they should be think they can survive because blame can be spread more widely. Teams can also be hiding places for managers to put under-performing employees with the hope that they will be able to contribute more as part of a team than they could individually. In the latter scenario, you as the manager are fooling yourself. Take care of the performance issue before putting the larger group or the project at risk.

I've never understood why people overload the team concept with such importance. It seems that some people are much more concerned about the structure of the project, group, or organization than the results. Don't make extra work for yourself; concentrate on the goals you want to achieve and then find the best people who can work together to achieve them.

Before assembling any "team," you must remember that the results will depend on the abilities of the individuals comprising the team. The best recipe for creating a solid, successful project team is to find good people and be very clear with them about precisely what their job is and what is expected from them, and then make sure that they understand what you've told them. But you can't just leave it at that. You must find a highly skilled, clever, and a meticulous coordinator to run this group of good people.

When you hear someone say, "we have our best team on it," be a bit cynical until you know who the individuals involved are. If all the individuals on this mythical team actually are the best individually skilled people in their disciplines and the individual coordinating the team is also the best, then that probably is the best team. Remember: the success of any collaborative project starts and ends with the individuals.

Let me give you an example. You have tasked Brian to develop a highly-sophisticated enterprise software solution that would marry numerous different technologies in novel ways. There would be cloud-based components, mobile interfaces, big data-crunching capabilities. You name it--the dreamers had piled the requirements high. On paper, it was all possible and the program manager, Brian, went about setting up the team structure and developed a list of the needed skills. After several weeks, he had the master plan. It was a great piece of work, very thoughtful and it presented very well.

So how confident should you be at this point? Through Brian's excellent work you have a clear set of requirements, you have a structure in place, you know all the disciplines you need to execute the work and know where you are going to get the people. You have an estimated time and budget and it appears rational for this early stage of the project. You have a list of risks and everyone is clear about them and onboard. Again, how confident should you be at this point?

Well, the program is launched and off you all go. There is a great buzz. People are excited and know this is a great program and they know the final product will be an industry leader, so spirits are high, in fact there is a great team spirit.

I maintain that nothing I have described so far can ensure success. I believe that success will come about if you can identify the list of individuals who have a higher level of skill and who will be able to steer the program's solution in the right direction. You also need to remove those who do not have the right skill level. So, success will be because of individual skills and not the team structure per se.

Chapter 15: Stress

You need to watch for signs of stress in yourself and in those who work at your company, because if it is not eliminated, or at least acknowledged and dealt with, there will be negative consequences. Some signs can be as simple and obvious as a greater tension between teams or shorter tempers in people who have never displayed them before. The situation can get more serious when people start avoiding places, tasks, or conversations, not doing the work they need to do, or missing days because they cannot face the stress of work.

The solution seems so simple: take away the sources of stress. Unfortunately, it is rarely possible to take away all sources of stress; in fact, it is often not simple to work out the underlying causes. In all businesses, there are many events and situations that can unnerve even the most seasoned employees. For instance, it might be an open secret that your company's industry is declining and it has you worried, but you are unsure if it will affect you. Perhaps business is booming and there is so much work needed to be done that no one is managing to keep up with all the tasks on their plate. It could be that people are time-slicing too much and their performance is suffering. Maybe an employee's partner or child is sick at home and he is worried all day long, but feels he cannot leave the office because there are some urgent deliverables.

These examples are only a sampling of situations that can give rise to stress. I am sure you can fill out pages and pages of others that you have experienced or have seen others experience. There are rarely easy solutions for any of these. The beginnings of stressful situations may have occurred far in the past and have just gradually built up to a point where a person shows outward signs of suffering. You can be certain that if your people are stressed, then the organization will also be negatively affected.

The critical thing is to be watchful and pay attention to your people and those around you. Use your common sense to determine what can cause stress and look for it in your company. Do you feel stressed yourself? If so, then you should expect others around you may also be affected. You must listen to what others are saying and be careful not to be dismissive just because *you* may be more immune to stress than they are.

Most importantly, as a manager or a colleague, you must look for ways to fix the issues that are causing stress. While it is not practical to assume that anyone can remove all sources of stress from a modern company or from anyone's life, it is possible to reduce the impact by taking some actions, such as stepping away physically and mentally from the situation for some "down-time" as regularly as you can, or talking about the situation with those around you or with a support group you have away from work. Educating yourself about the signs of stress and how it commonly impacts people is another crucial management skill that will be very helpful for you, your team, and for your company

I worked on a project in Hong Kong a number of years ago that was very complicated, very large, and business critical for the customer. We were replacing an existing installation with a totally new system that had to go live at the flick of a switch for more than 10,000 law enforcement users. Over several years, many teams worked independently on key designs and functionality that had to work seamlessly together or we would fail. The customer's expectations and our own were extremely high and we knew that, if we were successful, a lot of future business that would come our way from customers in many other parts of the world. So, no pressure really.

People were working seven days a week in the final push and, after a long stretch at this accelerated pace, I realized that I did not feel my usual sprightly self. I prided myself on never letting pressure get to me, but I felt less than my normal 100 percent. It took a few weeks of this before I realized something was up.

Pride can sometimes be a dangerous thing; luckily, I have enough of it but not a debilitating amount. I admitted to myself that I was under a lot of pressure and this was stressing my usual iron will. Filling every hour of my waking days, and sometimes nights, with the delivery of the project was a pattern I would need to break in order to clear my head for a bit and bring the stress level down. So, the next Sunday I jumped on a ferry to Lamma Island, landed on the northern point, and set out walking down the island. The day was Texas hot with Atlanta humidity. I had a few large bottles of water with me and a good pair of walking boots. I hiked around the island for the day and took in the scenery. It was a glorious day and about halfway through it I could feel myself relaxing.

The next day back at work I did feel better and refreshed, apart from my feet. The walk had distracted my brain and reduced the stress. I made it a habit to go on a walking adventure for one of the days each weekend. This worked very well for me and helped me do my part to successfully deliver the project while remaining sane.

So, be on the lookout for situations that are badly affecting your stress levels or those of your colleagues and teams. Find a practical way that works for you and your company to reduce the stress levels. The payback will be happier, more productive people and better performance for the company and your customers.

Chapter 16: Losing the Good Ones

I was at a going-away drinks party for one of the senior managers of our company. He was leaving voluntarily for a new opportunity and the managing director made a toast to the soon-to-be ex-employee. He said that it was unfortunate that Mr. T was leaving and wished him well. He went on the say that it is normally the case that only the good ones leave. While the rest of us in the group who were remaining with the company were not easily offended, this was not exactly a motivating speech.

Clearly, any company will be more successful competing against its rivals when it has a staff of brilliant, skilled people. There is no point denying that it is equally true that nothing stays the same forever and your company will lose what appears to be its most critical assets every so often. And even if you are in a company that does not have any formal

65

change program underway, change will happen by itself. Amazing that, really.

When people leave a company, there may be gaps left behind. This can be disruptive, but all that companies need to do to absorb the loss is to get on with filling the void. The good employees are often the more restless employees, and thoughts of where they can flourish better or earn more money or have a bigger position or more responsibility are never far from their minds. As a manager, you must accept the inevitability that you will lose some good people every now and then, and be ready for it. When they leave, thank them for their work in your company, learn exactly why they are going, and wish them good luck.

I also like to remind people that times do change and that if they decide they'd like to come back one day, there will be no penalty, no foul. (See, I can do sports stuff, too.) Good is good and every company will always want good people on its side.

You have all heard the stories told that "if So-and-so leaves the company or team, we are in big trouble; the projects will go down the tubes, and the customers will be unhappy and abandon us." Experience has taught every manager that there will be hiccups when people leave. However, it is rarely-to-never disruptive enough to bring a company, group, or project to its knees.

You have two choices when considering this inevitability: you can plan for it, or wait and handle it when it happens. I think that the latter may be what most people end up doing. Companies are so lean these days and there are so many "individual contributors" that you know you will get landed in difficulties if some of them were to leave. But, because money is not so freely flowing these days, few companies would allow you the financial flexibility to double up on the people you have identified as critical. The others around them are probably already so over-stretched that any idle thoughts you have about cross-training them are pure fantasy. So, whether you want to admit it or not, you are often times forced to live with the situation of not knowing if or when someone or several people might leave.

When that day comes, and the only person who understands that ancient computer system or has the combination to the safe or knows how to sweet-talk the client says they are leaving, you have no choice but to thank them, give them a good send off, and get on with the rest of your day. Do not be surprised to see the sun rising as usual the next morning.

People

Chapter 17: Stating and Questioning the Obvious

How many times have you been presented with a conclusion that comes with some very confident definitive statement such as 'We did all the research and the result is valid. We thought of everything and checked everything.' However, from your experience, the conclusion you are being presented does not *feel* right; it seems out of the ordinary and is setting off little alarm bells in your head. Your spider senses are tingling. What should you do? The work is done, the conclusion reached; should you just use the presented evidence or results and move on?

In such a situation, you are tempted to accept the conclusion because they must have thought of everything. You want to believe they were diligent, but the alarm bells going off in your head are letting you know that the conclusion just does not seem right. Again and again, across all

69

companies and situations, it turns out that the great investigators may not have actually thought of everything or may not have asked all the obvious questions and, in fact, the conclusion they reached on the topic is invalid, or at least incomplete.

You must always ask yourself whether the conclusion your team has reached passes your common-sense test. If there is any doubt in your mind about the conclusion or if the results seem out of the range of what is acceptable, then ask your questions. Ask for more details, or more research, or more answers. It is probably well worth the investment of their time to recheck the work, get another view, and question the information again.

My advice is not given because of my cynicism, although I am comfortable that I have a healthy level of cynicism. My advice is given because of my experience. Raise your hand if you recognize the following situation.

Your stomach drops and your heart skips a beat when your team of trusted professionals comes back to you after further study following your questions about their initial conclusion, and they tell you they now realize that their conclusion was actually wrong. Lo and behold, the new conclusion passes the common-sense test. Whereas they said something would work, it actually doesn't; when they said it would take a year, it now appears it will only be two months.

My personal story is along these lines. Having worked in a company for more than four years, I had gained a lot of knowledge about our suppliers' performance. Some were excellent and some less so. I had many years of lead-time data and had been using this history to plan all of our customer projects. One day, I was working on a complex, but not unusual, bid and the usual suspects were working on gathering delivery dates so I could finish the schedule.

A team member emailed me the information she had gathered for the lead time of the tanks and did not raise any special concerns about it. A few hours later, I was reviewing the information she supplied and I could see that the lead time was six months, instead of the normal two months. I picked up the phone and called her. We talked through the dates and she assured me that she did push the supplier on the dates and that there was nothing we could do to improve them.

Apart from the fact that our customers could not live with this extended delivery time, it was also highly unusual. I had two choices, accept the answer and the explanation I had been given, or dig into this apparent anomaly myself. I normally choose to dig. It takes time but, unfortunately, I normally find that there has been some breakdown in the communication that no one questioned sensibly. In the case of the delivery dates for the tanks, my team member had given the supplier a much higher specification for the material than was normal or needed and no one along the chain questioned it. The specifications for the tanks were revised to the normal tolerances and the supplier was then comfortable with the normal lead time.

Always remind people that if it does not sound sensible, then it probably is not and they need to thoroughly investigate and find the root cause. Too often, people searching for answers go only to a certain depth with their analysis because their drive is to reach a conclusion as soon as possible, especially if they know the conclusion they want to reach. They want the job finished and they want to get on with their lives, so they stop, present their findings, and convince themselves and others that they have done everything they could. People can be wrong and frequently are. You will end up making a mistake yourself if you do not question things when your instincts tell you to.

I'm frequently baffled as to why people approach problems with a closed mind and are blinded to results other than the result they expected, especially when they decided those were the results they wanted before they did the research. I'm equally baffled by people who are okay with declaring a problem unsolvable because they could not find the answer. In my opinion, people accept failure too easily and rationalize it away too easily. "I failed, but I tried hard" or "I gave it my best" are whiny, wishy-washy statements you hear regularly. You might have even uttered them yourself on occasion. It is hard to tease out of a person or team the things that have not been tried or the questions that were not asked, but you need to be watchful and diligent and ask the next round of questions.

Of course, you will find that the conclusions are not always wrong; in many cases, the hard work and thought that the team put into the study will be accurate. It is also only wishful thinking if you expect to be able to question the results and get the answer you were hoping for rather than the real answer. However, I have experienced too often the situation in which the conclusions were very wrong and a bit of diligent questioning caught the problem, so keep your eyes open and never be afraid to question yourself or your team when something feels out of whack.

People

Part II – The Job

People

Chapter 18: Results

Passing time idly can be a very pleasurable experience. How better to enjoy a warm summer's day when the sky is blue and there is a slow, cooling breeze? I recommend getting as much relaxation as you can when you can because idling results in restfulness and, often, happiness, which are worthwhile goals.

At work, there is a different drive and speed to life; there is the drive for good business results. The drive for results is critical to a business. If you have a team working for you, then earn your money by ensuring that the team achieves results. As a leader or manager, it is imperative that driving for results is a central theme of your cheerleader campaign—that it sets the mood and allows you to celebrate the behaviors that bring in the right results. Show your people how to achieve good results on a daily basis by setting a good example and pointing out others as good examples.

Everyone feels better when they achieve good results. It's incredibly satisfying to plan something and complete it, or reach a goal you set for yourself. One of the few things that can top this is praise for the same from someone you respect highly.

That being said, it is hard to drive for good results every single day of your working life, so do not try. You need to work hard and diligently, earn your pay, but understand that everyone needs some downtime. You will never be able to maintain 100 percent perfection or a never-ending drive for the best results. When planning any campaign, you must include some breathing space, so that you and your team will be most effective for the longer term. It is truly amazing what humans can achieve and how high a level of effort can be sustained for prolonged times, but there are limits and you never want to find those limits just before you are expected to deliver that career-saving or career-advancing customer order.

Be realistic when you make plans and allow time for resolving the numerous unknowns and problems you will encounter. State your doubts and admit the risks, then think about how to address them when you are faced with them. The actions you end up taking will probably be much different than those you had in mind at the first blush of planning but, because you have at least thrown it into the chaos of your thought processes ahead of time, a solution will be found more easily when you need it.

We are all guilty of losing the plot every now and then, and it does not hurt to be reminded that there are good reasons why a company exists and to be reminded that there should be a point to all of the sometimes-random activity you see all about you every day.

All companies operate in the social environment, but are normally not focused on providing "a better life" to their employees nor are they focused on providing job security for their employees. Business is volatile; no company is in a position to make long-term guarantees or predictions. So, why does the for-profit company exist? Hold on, I think I see a hint here. Is it so that some profits are made? Well done. The company exists to make a profit for its owners or shareholders by producing products or providing services that customers find valuable enough to buy at a price that is comfortably above the costs involved.

It's worthwhile to occasionally remind everyone in the company of precisely what the desired end result of their work is, as well as the simple reality that they get paid to achieve, accordingly, the generation of profits—period. The pursuit of profits does not imply abuse of the people needed to achieve those profits.

You are the manager and a key part of your job is to remind people constantly that the business needs to achieve good results regularly, which means the teams driving the business must consistently achieve good results. A business will never achieve its full potential without a group of like-minded, results-driven individuals doing what they need to do and doing it well.

It is all about results. Better still if they are good results. What is crucial to achieving them is to drive hard when needed, but also remember that you and your team will need to plan time to recover both physically and mentally before the next big push.

Chapter 19: Balancing the 3 Ps

The three Ps I refer to in this chapter are possibility, practicality, and profitability.

Running a business is a continuous 3P balancing act. That means, to be a successful leader, you must not only possess the ability to do this, you must become adept at it. It's a hard-earned talent. As your skills and intuition at balancing the three Ps improve, you can expect your company to recognize this and your career to benefit greatly.

I have spent a lot of time trying to find a clear way to communicate the dynamics and major levers of the 3P balancing act, specifically how they need to balance and what happens if any of the balance points are not aligned properly. One day, while trying to rationalize and solve a challenge put to my team about a new product, I settled on the first point of balance: the art of the possible. Our challenge was to answer whether it was possible to engineer an enhanced feature for a product. The situation being considered was not simple and the answer would take some days to get to a preliminary conclusion. The team analyzed the challenge, gathered information, and consulted with many technical experts in the hope of finding the answer. Two days later, the team decided it was possible—because anything was possible.

That made the challenger happy. The team members were thanked for their efforts and the powers that be moved on to make their next decision. However, my inclination was to say *hold on a minute. Stop right there before you go any further. Is that all you are going to ask?*

No one had yet asked if it would be practical to create the new feature. Whether some great new idea will be practical very much depends on its full scope, how it ranks against all the other things that need to be done or can be done, and whether there are the right resources—people, as well as funding—available to apply to it. The question needs to be asked whether this is the right time and stage of the company's journey to attempt this task, even if it is *possible* to do it. Do not get me wrong, I am not suggesting that the default should be to shy away from challenges. Far from it—a competitive company must be challenging its people all the time. It is common knowledge that if a team really puts their minds and resources behind something, there is a very good chance of achieving the goal. However, the practicality of an endeavor is equally as important a consideration as whether it is possible.

Now that the possibility and the practicality of a solution have been addressed, the third P needs to be added to the discussion. The expected response, you might be thinking, is that if the end-result cannot be profitable, then the goal will be out of balance and we are in the danger zone. After all, we are all in business to make money for the company owners and ourselves, so garnering a positive and rapid profit must always be the right answer to the profit question. However, in practice, investing resources to achieve a goal that does not deliver an immediate profit, but rather provides the expectation of profit at a later date, either directly through this work or indirectly through a related revenue stream, is a sound decision. In either case, profitability is the final balancing point and is crucial to the success of an endeavor.

We need to balance the three Ps and not take them in isolation. In some companies, there are different teams who consider these balancing points independently. In such cases, the collective can end up making a potentially damaging mistake, unless there is good coordination and a clear realization of the connection between the teams. Instead, train your full team to drive each other to balance the business decisions, to be aware of the pitfalls, and to make the correct choices.

Examples of out-of-balance decisions are unfortunately common. Take the case of a hard-working, driven salesperson who sees all sorts of possibilities to win more customers with new or enhanced products. She goes to the equally enthusiastic engineering team with a great challenge: help the customers by adding a stronger container for the equipment. After serious deliberation, the engineering team declares that it is both possible and a great idea. Yes, they addressed the art of the possible, but then someone remembered that they had planned to change three other features. The budget could not accommodate the new plan, and so would force a choice. The team and the salesperson had to hit the brakes and balance the practicality of the new plan with the art of the possible. This situation naturally led to the tie-breaker: which feature or features would be the most profitable in the end? If they had stopped their due diligence by only looking at one aspect of the three Ps, they would probably end up selling a great, enhanced product that may have cost more to make with no improvement in profit margin or, worse still, a reduced margin.

Balancing the three Ps—the art of the possible, a clear view on practicality, and a razor-sharp focus on profitability—are difficult and daily decisions faced by many, if not most, businesses. But, if you get the balance right and find a way to streamline the decision processes to reach the conclusion as efficiently as possible, the decision to go ahead or not to go ahead will pay off financially. It has an added benefit of motivating your teams, who will be part of an organization that is balanced and making great choices for its customers and its future.

Chapter 20: Dealing with Customers

Customers are people, too.

That statement may sound stupid, but it's true — and they come with many different personalities, just like the range of people you see in your own company and life.

It is always important to identify the type of customer you are dealing with in any particular transaction. Some are good, some are bad, some are friendly, some are shouters, and, while you may think that your dealings with them are very important, you are likely only one of many priorities your customers are balancing. There are those customers who want to be helpful and have things succeed, those who do not want to get blamed by their own company for anything that might possibly go wrong with an order or project and will throw you under the bus without hesitation, and those who think being loud and obnoxious is a good way to be. (Hint: it is not).

It's important to study your customers to learn what they are like and how to please them. It's natural to want to jettison the bad ones that demand a high price for their custom. But be careful not to be too arrogant because it will be a rare occasion when you are in a position to be so choosy.

It's almost part of the business landscape that sometimes, maybe frequently, people get so tied up in their own blinkered worlds that they forget that the real reason a for-profit business exists is to provide a service or product to a paying customer. Many people think that their job is to perform a specific task and it is somebody else's job to make sure the puzzle pieces fit together to make a customer happy. This limited view and attitude is short-sighted and needs prompt attention. If you, as the manager, see this attitude being adopted internally, the customer can probably see it, too. And might see more than you would like them to see.

Every employee in a company must understand the needs of the customers and be ready and able to help satisfy all but the most extreme. If they don't understand this, you might need to point out that all of your employees are customers of other businesses, whether it is the various restaurants they frequent or the telephone company that they use. Your employees know when they get good or bad service, and when they are being reasonable or unreasonable. Just as individuals continually rate the service they get throughout their days, companies assess the service they receive. Ensure your teams take to heart the approach to your company's customers that treats the customer the same way the employee would like to be treated

People

Chapter 21: Informational Meetings

How to effectively communicate with people has been a topic of much study at least since communication was born. History describes a continuum of communications problems. My personal history includes many discussions about how best to communicate in business and what forms of communication will ensure that the proper information gets through to the intended audience. And not just gets through to the right people, but ensures that those people hear and understand the messages, and act on them in the way the company needs them to do.

Even after all this time and effort—centuries of it—achieving good means of communication is a challenge. Some companies have endless "all-hands" meetings, which are intended to reach as many people as possible at the same time. These all-hands calls can be helpful, but I have seen too many situations in which few people are actually paying attention to the information in such calls because the information being shared is not of interest to them. This shouldn't come as a surprise. There is that old adage about "you can't please all of the people all of the time." Well, it's damned hard to interest all of the people all of the time, too, even if they all have a common interest, such as how the company that pays them a salary is doing. One would think that if, for instance, a call is about the current state of the business and the things that will be the focus of everyone's attention for the next three to six months that would be considered critical information. Unfortunately, many people attending these high-level calls struggle to relate the information to actions they need to take or the impact the information might have on them.

While battling with the best way to communicate to individuals on these calls, there is still some important general information that you will need to share with all: Is the company making money? Are our customers happy? Is the work environment safe? What good things happened recently? What bad things happened recently?

I've found a few remedies to ensure my meetings are effective. I keep them short, 45 minutes at most, but 15 minutes is better, and I invite everyone who might need to be there. I realize that sounds like a contradiction to what I said earlier, but it's one of those sad-but-true situations. There are times when everyone needs to be invited because there will be a perceived divide between the 'insiders' and the 'rest of us,' if you do not. So, although it is foolish, sometimes it is more simple and effective in the long-term to invite all, in order to disarm some people who might get disgruntled at not being invited. I have also seen it effectively shorten the communication cycle because all the key participants are present and can answer questions on the spot. Again, I stress that brevity is best.

You will never be able to talk directly to everyone at once, so make sure that the people who cannot attend your communications call get the information you want to share. This might mean sending a list of the actions you need them to take, or having those who did attend host follow-on meetings to pass the word along, or issuing a newsletter, email, or other distributed communique. If your company is a large multinational that has people and offices spread across many countries and time zones, communicating your message effectively and simultaneously to everyone who needs to be aware of it is even more difficult. You will need to rely on your managers to interpret and communicate the core messages, so make sure to give them very clear directions or a cheat sheet to use in their follow-on communications.

Another brave idea for the informational meetings you will have on a regular basis is to ask people what they want to hear. I mean what subjects, not the actual answers, although if you find out what answers they want to hear, you may learn something about the state of mind of your employees. There are those in every organization that want only a warm and fuzzy feeling from their CEO or manager. Others want very detailed data to understand what is going on. There are many others on the spectrum in between these two extremes. In any case, this is our audience and your job is to get through to as many as you can.

Meetings are held for many purposes, for sharing general or specific information, and for sharing good news and, at times, bad news. You need to have different techniques for running each kind of meeting. There is no magic formula and you will get so many conflicting opinions on 'the right way' to communicate that your head would explode if you tried to pick the one and only way. Some people are naturally great communicators; the rest of us need to be thoughtful and learn how to improve our communications at every opportunity.

I find that during every meeting, I manage to learn a bit more about communicating effectively. One all-hands meeting I hosted is a case in point. Historically, these meetings involve me sharing a range of financial updates about how the business is doing, who has joined or left us recently, orders, customer activity—the usual. It was mostly *The Richard Smith Show*. However, on this day I had decided that others should also present and one of these great folks was sharing our initiative to strengthen our health and safety record. My style was to stand at the end of the room and try and be loud enough so all those hiding down the back could hear, while hers was to walk around the room between the tables and get closer to more people. I was a bit stiff, not too much; she was definitely more fluid. Our styles could not have been more different.

I thought the meeting went well. Afterward, some people approached me with feedback on how they thought it went. The feedback was very interesting. Some people thought I was great and that only about half the audience was asleep. Others thought that our EHS presenter was great and that the other half of the audience was asleep. It was confirmation that different people can be engaged in different ways; in fact, they *need* to be engaged differently, if you are going to get through to them. So, I managed to reach half the audience and she managed to reach half the audience. That is 100 percent coverage in my meeting math.

One-on-one communication has many challenges, larger group communication has another set. I would encourage you to experiment, try some different formats, get feedback, adjust, practice, ask for help, add players to the troupe. These large groups meetings can be very powerful, if done well, and, just like Stella, finding your grove will you lift your spirits and make you a more effective communicator.

People

Chapter 22: Presentation Skills

It is almost a rite of passage that, at some point early in your professional career, you will be expected to prepare a presentation. The first few presentations, and perhaps all, for some people, are typically met with dread. For some, it is the thought of speaking in public that induces that chaotic churn in the gut and the gray matter. For others, it is the realization that their intellectual, planning, or execution skills will be on full display — or not, as the case may be. For still others, it could be the fear of being boring. My biggest issue with presentations is the fear of being bored senseless, even by ones I create.

It should come as no surprise that I have a strong opinion about presentations. Simply put, I think many, and probably most, are brilliant examples of time and talent wasted in pursuit of ... more time and talent being wasted. People generally take a lot of time putting them together, trying to ensure they are on-point, attractive, and entertaining, when all they really have to be is informative. I ask you: wouldn't it be great if all presentations were recitations of just the relevant information needed to develop a plan, make a decision, or whatever other action needed to be taken?

It is important to be able to discern when and how to put forth your best efforts into a presentation and when to punt, all the while maintaining your sanity. The one caveat here is that I'm primarily addressing internal presentations. Customer-facing presentations are a different species and require a different approach, although I have not yet met a customer who does not appreciate brevity and clear factual content.

My first rule is that, if you believe that a particular presentation is really a waste of time and effort, then you should try to convince the person expecting you to give the presentation that it's wasteful and suggest a better way to communicate the message—maybe a call, a face-to-face meeting, a short email, or even a tweet. If your powers of persuasion fail you, then just relax.

Yes, you read that correctly. Relax and leave things until closer to the last minute. Granted, it may not be natural for you, but it is a great time-saver. My reasoning is this: the presentations created for internal business use will only ever be seen once, if you are lucky. In fact, it is highly likely that only one-tenth of what you might produce will ever achieve glory by being projected onto a wall or displayed on a screen. Not even the Bing (or Google, if that is still around) search engine will ever find anything anyone is interested in past Slide 10 on a PowerPoint slide deck, even if the slide is titled *"Free Money! Get your hands on it without doing anything. Guaranteed!!!"*

When you finally sit down to pull it together, adhere to Rule #2: presentations should be short and sweet and get to the point right away. Make sure you have data available to support your points, even though you know that the data are never likely to see the light of a projector.

My third rule: no music or animation. Ever. It has taken many decades but, thankfully, animation in presentations is finally frowned upon. This saves a significant amount of time and the occasional embarrassment of that errant click meant to slide the final bullet point into place but that was, in fact, one click too many and, *voilà*, the next slide appears early. Now, you are backtracking to get to where you expected to be. Let's leave the animation to Pixar, shall we? Take the time you would have spent doing Disney proud and focus instead on being sharp on the day.

My next rule—am I up to 10 yet?—is that what you have on the slides is nowhere near as important as is paying attention to your audience and adjusting to their reactions. Don't allow yourself, out of fear or ego, to become so absorbed in your headings and bullet points that you lose your audience. If you start to see or hear side conversations start up, you need to pause and ask if there is question you can answer. If people start asking questions about topics you will cover 10 slides forward, you need to decide quickly whether to deflect the question until you get to that slide or discard your deck order and leap forward.

Presentations will always be dynamic situations, inevitably attended by a group of people who each are only interested in a fraction of the whole that you need to impart. So be ready, relax, and adjust as you go.

I acknowledge that not everyone will be comfortable preparing for a meeting in a last-minute fashion; it takes experience to be able to accurately assess the needs of the audience and only prepare what is truly needed. You need to know a few things in advance, namely: the interest level of the audience members; whether they really care to hear from you; whether the issue is still hot or if a decision has been made and you are part of a play contrived to show process in action; or whether your part is just to have something for the record, despite what you may have been told. You need to understand these things because you do not want to be wasting your precious time creating slides that no one needs or reads.

I admit I am being more than a bit flippant, but we have all been in those meetings where the 50-slide presentation only got to Slide 4 or 5 after an hour, and then more time had to be scheduled for another day to finish the meeting. It happens all too frequently and is a colossal waste of time and talent that no company can afford to waste.

For all presentations, I suggest that you start with a summary of what was learned in your research or what decisions need to be made. Get to the point at the start. Next, include a brief overview of the evidence you have or process you followed to support your message. This is a good point to pause for a conversation to see if anyone needs clarification or more details. Quite often, if the summary and evidence are strong enough, then the meeting can conclude and you will have achieved the goal.

So, take a short cut to a more productive work life and cut down your presentation excesses. You will not regret it. See Slide 73, Point3a.1 if you do not believe me.

People

Chapter 23: Managing Resource Constraints

It's not a long bet that you are familiar with the excuse that your company/department/organization has too many things to do and not enough people to get those things done in good time. And that the solution is to get more people working on the issue at hand ASAP. What I've discovered is that, in most situations, there are enough people to do what needs to be done. The real problem is usually that people waste time on activities that are of limited, questionable, or no value.

Think about the many wasteful tasks being diligently performed around you, and then consider what the result would be if they were eliminated or severely curtailed. Chances are your team would end up with the ability and time to do other things. When you meet with your

CEO about resources, bring your functioning brain with you; bring options and ideas, instead of a request for more people.

Wherever the resource constraint, first ask yourself and your team if every task you are doing contributes value to the project. Ask whether it is required to meet a customer's need or to support activities for meeting future customer needs. Ask whether it is necessary to attain or maintain compliance with some legal requirement or regulation. You know from experience that there will be waste, and part of your job is to find it and remove it.

After you have done your homework and the waste has been addressed, there remains a need to expand the resources to get the jobs done. Now is the time to bring your case to the company. Bring clear evidence to support any shortages you have and identify the financial benefits that adding people will provide. Remember that you will be presenting a case to someone who cannot be as intimately involved in the details of your group as you are, so the person on the other side of the desk will struggle to divine whether your needs are real and whether your solutions are the right ones. At this stage, you need to be clear. Support your case with good, easy-to-digest data, your summary spreadsheet, and maybe one or two slides, and go get the needed resources.

Even if you get your request rubber-stamped, you need to accept that ramping up new resources takes a long time and you will not see the benefits for days, weeks, or sometimes months later, depending on your situation.

Working within a multitude of constraints, such as time, money, or resources, is a reality that never goes away, and it is a key part of a manager's role to understand those constraints, predict them when possible, cleverly and quickly analyze solutions, and build a case to convince the leadership of the need and the possible outcomes. Then, all that remains is to do the work.

People

Chapter 24: Be a F.O.R.C.E of Nature: The Secret Sauce in Effective Project Management

There are some great resources that explain the how-to of project and program management with tomes written from the highest-level concepts to the most intricate details. My aim is to teach you all you need to know about project management in two or three paragraphs. I can hear you howling with either laughter or disgust—what a fool you say, how dare you! I have had a lot of experience managing hundreds of projects, both directly myself or through others, so I have a strong basis to back my approach. Even more importantly, I have been involved in projects that succeeded and projects that, in my opinion, failed. I am happy to report that the successes far outweigh the failures, but I learned much from each.

105

The difference between a program manager and a project manager can get blurred in many companies, so I will define the terms as I am going to be using them. I define a *project* manager is a person who is responsible for executing a part of an overall program. A *program* manager be an executive, a floor manager, or someone else in a position of responsibility who may or may not be trained in the project management disciplines, but who is running the overall program, which might include one or more distinct or connected projects. As such, the program manager typically has a wider set of responsibilities than the project manager, including the unenviable role of managing all the stakeholders connected to the project(s) under his or her control. The program manager ordinarily has one or more project managers to help run the projects.

So much for the preamble. Let's get to the key skills project managers need to succeed and consistently achieve good results. (Program managers, you don't have to stop reading this chapter. Read it so you can suggest these tips to your project managers.)

You may not believe me, but it wasn't until after I wrote down these key attributes and skills that I realized if I re-ordered them slightly the acronym F.O.R.C.E appeared. I think it works, in the sense of "F.O.R.C.E." as a force of nature, a personality of great strength, energy, and/or intensity. The F.O.R.C.E. attributes are:

Be *Flexible* – be prepared for the changes that will happen and handle them when they do.

Be *Organized* – make lists and schedules, work them, adhere to them, and rely on them.

Be *Realistic* – don't fool yourself or let yourself be fooled.

Be a great *Communicator* – this applies to both the quantity and quality of what you produce.

Be *Energetic* – have the energy to succeed, to drive the team, be the cheerleader, set the pace.

Be Flexible

Things change all the time. While you should try to foresee all changes, this never can be fully achieved, so be ready, willing, and able to deal with change in a professional manner. The magic is to manage the changes smoothly while keeping the project moving forward at a good pace. Prepare the team at the start for changes, set the cultural expectations, and be very clear how changes will be reviewed, analyzed, and handled.

Be Organized

You cannot run a project using a set of email chains. Make lists and make sure every task on each list has a clear owner, end date, and verification plan. A significant key to success is to get team agreement documented so that people take personal accountability. Efficiently run through the lists in appropriately-sized groups during effectively run meetings. Publish the lists in a known place, such as the project folder maintained on the network, so that they are readily available for review and reference. This will help to ensure there is the one and only version of the truth. As project manager, you should lead by example: be on time, be organized, and show everyone that you expect the project and the project team to mimic your behavior.

Be Realistic

A company will get the most benefit from a project that is delivering its goals in a timely manner, by which I mean as soon as possible. As project manager, ensure you do not fall into the trap of setting easy goals because you are being 'realistic.' The modern business world, with its inherent level of competition, requires speed. Being realistic means that you need to be intimate with the dynamics of your projects and your environment, that you can't assume success, and you can't passively set or agree to goals that you cannot deliver. Be realistic about the talents you have and the talents the team has, and make any needed changes as early as possible in the project. Be realistic, but also be aware that a project with too much buffer in the schedule likely means you are going slower than the competition and may lose out by being too slow to market.

Be a Great Communicator

Our human ability to communicate both in writing and verbally is a skill set that no other creature on earth possesses, yet it is too often one of our weakest skill sets. It takes effort, but not extraordinary effort, to overcome this weakness and improve your communication skills.

The successful project manager will work each day to communicate as clearly as possible to as many of the project team members as needed. PMs generally need to communicate up, down, and sideways at the same time and in the most appropriate way for the different audiences and people. Since people interpret the exact same words differently depending on the tone in which the words are said (or written, in the case of email), the mood the person is in when hearing the words, and what the person actually wants to hear or interpret, clear communication is by far the greatest challenge a PM faces. Those who master this skill will be more successful. So, continually let everyone know what is going on and remind them of their part in making the endeavor successful.

Be Energetic.

People will take their lead from the leader. There are days when you are up and there are days you are down, but those who are at the top of this game, those who are a F.O.R.C.E. of nature, keep the low-energy states to themselves and consistently show the team a higher-energy version. There will be some downtime in the life of a project and you need to inject some time for the teams to blow off steam and have some fun, particularly on lengthy projects. Just like you need to sleep at night and go into a lower state in order to have the energy for the next day, this natural cycle will be mimicked in any project, so find a way to build it in, find a way to plan for it. A higher level of energy and passion from the project lead will result in a higher performing team, a happier team, and a better outcome for the project. So, eat your spinach regularly.

To recap, when you become a F.O.R.C.E of nature, you and your projects will be more successful.

- Be Flexible
- Be Organized
- Be Realistic
- Be a Great Communicator
- Be Energetic

Part III – The Games

People

Chapter 25: Ladders and Other Dangerous Things

To climb or not to climb the corporate ladder: that is the question.

The first time I was given a promotion into the leadership group of a company, the person whose place I was taking told me that I should "prepare to be underwhelmed." For a while, I thought he was right; however, I discovered that there were some sparks of life in the leadership team. It is true that the dynamics change as you climb the ladder in an organization and what was easy at a smaller group level can become much more complex at a higher level.

Take, for example, decision-making. You might have been your own boss, more or less, at a lower level and had a significant amount of influence over how well you or your group implemented your decisions.

The reality is that, as you move higher up in the organization, even the apparently simple decisions have a limited chance of moving from the drawing board to the real world and having a fruitful life. Yes, I said a fruitful life—meaning that it would be a worthy and respected decision that spawned successful offspring and retired only after it completely met its highest goals. Unfortunately, too often decisions become the orphaned children of a hastily called and poorly executed session that leaves everyone, including the decision, unsatisfied. From such a start, life for a decision can never be anything other than bleak.

My example of decision-making at higher levels in an organization is just one of many aspects of change you need to be prepared for as you grow in a company and take on larger roles with more responsibility.

So, about that ladder. The first rung is deciding what you want to do over the next few years. When you've done that and are ready to take the second step—stepping up with both feet, so to speak—you need to make a plan. It does not need much detail, but it needs to include something along the lines of "I will work to become responsible for a bigger slice of our business over the next 12 months" or something suitably worthy and achievable.

There is a simple equation that directly relates pay to hassle. (In some quarters, it's known as the STP Ratio: Shit-to-Pay.) If you want more money, then be prepared to give up some things, such as some of the free time you have come to expect and enjoy, vacations uninterrupted by phone calls, worry-free weekends. This is the hassle part. However, there are also benefits that accompany those hassles and those are part of the reason you would want to start the climb in the first place. Being a leader in an organization is fun and rewarding. You get to be part of the solutions and decisions, and, therefore, not as blind to the reasoning behind them.

For some people getting to the top of the ladder is the end-goal and the journey is fueled by an internal drive to be the top dog, to have power and control. This kind of person will undertake the climb with little or no regard for those around them. They will not think twice of climbing over someone who is ahead of them on the ladder, if the opportunity arises, or to step on the hands of those coming up behind them. It's all about winning for those people, and how they play the game doesn't matter at all. So much for the words of every Little League coach ever.

Some people call this type of person a sociopath, others would use the term "asshole." Lots of people call this kind of person "the boss." My opinion, if it's not already crystal clear, is that these are not good people to be around, whether you work with them or for them, or they work for you, and companies where they thrive are not companies worth working for.

Ambition is a great thing to have and to exercise, and I do not object to it in any way. But, I do object to blind ambition as I have described it here. It's addictive to people who gets a taste of it, and becomes toxic and pervasive in every situation they inhabit. The very good news is that there are not too many of these crazies out there, but be on the lookout for them because they can make life at the top, middle, and bottom very unpleasant.

When you rise above some of your former peers, you will be seen as a changed person. It's a fair observation, because things will be different and so will you. You will have to treat people differently because you have so much more information and some of it might be related to your former peers. You will not, however, be *very* different, unless you choose to be. If, on your climb, you were only pretending to be a nice person and the acquisition of your new power allowed people to see that you are actually an asshole, then you will not have changed, because you were always an asshole. The only thing that's different is that your true colors are shining through.

Do not get offended if someone says to you that you used to be fun, but now you are serious. Your changed demeanor is a result of the fact that you most likely have taken on more work, are possibly a part of some very serious discussions and decisions, and have a new responsibility to think about the business from a broader perspective. You will appear yet more serious at budget time because you are a part of the team, or maybe the only person, who needs to decide what staffing levels you can afford to maintain based on the year ahead. This is relatively easy if the year looks better than last, and a disaster (and serious) if the prediction is that there will be less money coming in.

I have seen an increasing number of people who have risen to a level in their careers where they are happy with what they have and do not need or want to go to the next level. It took me a while to understand that this is not due to a lack of ambition or some other issue, but that they have reached the perfect place for themselves. Too many people don't think it through to this stage, though. Here's the secret: every company needs these core people as stabilizing forces.

I once achieved the corner office. It was nice. It was big, and had huge windows, a conference table, and a private bathroom. I moved out of it after a few months because all those windows made it unbearably hot in the summer, even with the air conditioning going, and cold in the winter, even with the heat on. I couldn't heat or cool the entire building just to suit the atmosphere in my office, because I had to pay the bills (and because I'm not one of *those* bosses). And you know what else? I never used the private bathroom. Think about it for a minute. Having it right there made it more awkward than convenient. Some of my questions included: Was the ventilation appropriate? What about sounds—did they travel? If I used it, was it proper etiquette to shut my office door first, or did I want to risk coming out of it, only to find people waiting for me in my office and not knowing how long they'd been there, or what they'd been doing. Would I have to lock my computer for the duration of every visit, no matter how quick? These were hassles I didn't need. When I moved out of the office, I turned the space into a break room and let the staff determine how best to use the "executive washroom" because this executive never did.

There are benefits to ladder-climbing, such as a better view, and there are sacrifices, such as living with a greater weight on your shoulders. Just remember to read the warning signs as you go, and make sure you know what you are getting into and that you want to get into

117

it. Keep climbing for as long as the rewards outnumber the drawbacks, and then stop.

Chapter 26: Politics at Work – Game Playing

Do not play politics or games at work. Just don't.

I say this because you are an ass if you do, and obviously just a self-serving fool. Of course, maybe you're a natural-born political animal and you think playing games is the right approach; if you are such a person, I'm surprised you made it this far into this book. And, by the way, I do not like your type.

Ok, so you are still reading and count yourself as someone who is straightforward and honest. You still need to be diligent and avoid anyone who is not straightforward. Those folks can and will cause harm to you or other decent people around you at some point and you most likely won't see it coming. There is a difference between the political

119

animals I'm talking about in this chapter and people who are genuinely clever, understand the institution, and do things that benefit the customer *and themselves*. There is no harm in that. The animal to avoid is the person who only cares about benefits to him- or herself.

You see, the primary and sole intention of the political beast is to twist the circumstance to suit his or her own situation and, if you are in the way, the beast will not hesitate to dispatch your good name in pursuit of the goal. There are many levels of talent in all disciplines and the political beast covers the spectrum from amateur to ninja. The amateurs are dangerous because they blunder their way through, leaving tasks and reputations in random tatters. Ninjas tend to jump out of nowhere unexpectedly and kill all about them quickly and before you can figure out what's going on. Don't ignore the amateurs, but the ninjas are the one you need to keep an eye on — if you can spot them.

If you cannot avoid these political beasts, and often you can't, you need to determine what agenda they are pushing or what goal they have in mind, and then come up with a subtle plan to thwart them. You need to give them enough rope to hang themselves because … why not? If nothing else, you will get some entertainment out of it. Just be very careful and do not play this game unless you are prepared to get burnt; these people can be very clever, spiteful, and not a little vicious. Think sociopath — a person with no conscience and no shame who, in the words of Alexander Pope, is delighted to

> Damn with faint praise, assent with civil leer,
> And without sneering, teach the rest to sneer;

120

Willing to wound, and yet afraid to strike,
Just hint a fault, and hesitate dislike.

Let's consider the case of Mary, Mike, and Karl. They had been working together for more than five years on many combined initiatives, as well as on independent assignments. Vicki was their boss and she was a straight shooter. Work was fairly predictable; there were some great team successes, some individual successes, and some other less successful projects. The dynamics of this Terrific Trio was tense at times, but the group appeared to have a good self-balancing mechanism. There was mutual respect.

Vicki called her team into a conference room one Friday and told everyone that she was being promoted, she needed to choose a successor for her current job, and they were all eligible to apply. Within two weeks, the team had destroyed their relationship and none of them got the job. A new person was hired from outside.

Here's what happened: Mike had been biding his time, and with the possible promotion now in play, he showed his true political colors. He had lived through the ups and down of the team, recording every failure of his peers, in detail, as well as developing what he thought were clear rebuttals to any challenges were made to his own failures. Of course, Mike also had a great story about his true leadership skills and how he had carried the others during all of their successes. Mike launched his campaign the minute Karl and Mary left the meeting at which Vicki announced the upcoming changes.

Mike told Vicki how excited he was to see her advance and said if he could ever do anything to help, he was ready, willing, and able. Over the next few weeks, Mike didn't miss an opportunity to share with Vicki his revisionist, self-flattering version of the group history. He was extremely helpful in explaining why certain things had failed in the past and how Mary and Karl had "done their best in difficult circumstances."

Needless to say, Mary and Karl could see what Mike was up to, but Mike was so engorged with ambition that he brushed them off when they directly confronted him and just continued his political campaign; he was going to get the promotion at all costs.

Vicki was no idiot and was appalled by Mike's actions, but she also assumed that Mary and Karl had a role in this game. In the end, they all lost out; one was guilty and deserved it, and the other two were caught in the crossfire.

Political games at work are a waste of your energy, a waste of your work and personal time and, therefore, a waste of the organization's money. You cannot trust anyone who plays political games in an organization because, if they play games with other people, they will eventually play them with you. This is, without doubt, a most critical thing to know and remember.

Chapter 27: Passive Aggression

I was either lucky or blind because it was only after about 15 years spent working in a number of different companies that I began to see people who purposefully acted in a passive-aggressive way. I'm a person who expects people to be decent by default and am continually surprised by the childish, vindictive behavior some people consider acceptable. Watch out for the people who behave that way, the people who enable it, and the people who condone it. They are all dangerous. If you are one of them, stop it. I've seen the best teams in the business taken down when someone who is passive-aggressive used his talents against the team, and his strategy was not caught in time. It is inevitably ugly and inevitably painful.

You need to find these aggressors in your organization and take the wind out of their sails. If left alone, they'll spend time and money accomplishing precisely nothing, and when the time is right for the maximum disruptive effect, they'll spring the glorious news of how they tried very hard, but could not get their job done in time. Such people always seem to be deeply unhappy creatures who thrive on creating churn and the negative energy it creates. Some choice descriptions come to mind when I think of these people: Bastards. Selfish fools. Emotional vampires. Small-minded, petty pricks.

Vent if you need to, when you encounter them, but track their actions clearly and review them publicly as they happen. Sunshine is the best cure for their disease. Like roaches, they will find another dark place to hide very quickly.

Sometimes, these people are found quite high up in companies and I've often wondered how they survived for that long. This is an important issue to ponder. Even if you ignore the damage these people do to your customers and other workers, you have to wonder how they always manage to make it to the end of another week. Clearly, these passive aggressors have their own demons and there is a character flaw at work. You cannot change this, so do not waste your energy trying to fix them, educate them, or reform them. Instead, you must work out what element of your organization or its culture or management practices allows the passive aggressors to keep their jobs. Once you have worked it out, be the one to fix it.

Chapter 28: Will All The Assholes Please Stand Up?

It is amazing how effective a direct call for the assholes to identify themselves can be. If you ask them to identify themselves, they will. Without fail. And usually quite quickly.

Maybe a "direct call" isn't quite the right phrasing. I'm not suggesting anyone stand up on a chair in the middle of the office and shout, "Will all the assholes please stand up?", although it's a tempting prospect, isn't it? Rather, I'm suggesting that you pay attention and stay alert. Every day in every company, there are many opportunities to observe people in action and, if you watch closely, the assholes will always make themselves known.

Now, I'm not talking about people who are just negative or even chronically negative, nor the political or chronically political. It's more than that. You can be negative, but not an asshole, and you can be a very political person, but not an asshole. The assholes are those people who do not want to be helpful, who treat others' opinion or actions with undeserved disrespect, who are rude, who you would sometimes call bullies, who have it all worked out and tell you that you do not, who are obviously and publicly sucking up to the senior managers. I could go on. I won't.

Avoid them or learn how to handle them by giving them every opportunity to expose their true selves, which will ensure that all those around the assholes are forewarned. If you are skilled enough, try to screw them subtly for entertainment. There isn't much of a downside to the latter. Assholes are not as dangerous as the political sociopath because they are frequently less than clever but, thanks to their super-sized egos, they are not aware of that. If you are lucky enough to be around when they finally figure out what you're doing, your sense of satisfaction will increase exponentially.

Chapter 29: Going Up – The Escalation Culture

Maybe you've encountered this situation: the customer has asked you for a long list of information and needs it sooner than you can deliver it. You're very professional and politely tell the customer that you will get them the information but that it will take you longer than they have requested. You can tell that the customer just will not accept that answer and they will probably be making a call very soon. I've seen this situation plenty of times and can usually tell when someone is about to deploy the "direct escalation" approach. You know what it is. Maybe you've even done it. The mechanism is simple. You call the big boss, convey the urgency of the situation, and sit back and watch the process work. Requests become demands, organized approaches become chaotic, relationships are badly damaged, frustration levels spike.

I expect that you have all come across this type of situation in your daily work. You know it is the wrong way to do things and that, in the end, the business suffers. Yet, you still do it.

The escalation culture is bad on so many levels. For openers, as a manager, you have just put yourself in the ridiculous position of having surrendered control — *control that is part of what you are paid to maintain.* Your boss is not going to be happy about this, either, because he or she is now distracted by something the "team" (that means *you*) should be able to handle. The next step is for the boss to begin to doubt the organization. (That also means *you*.)

There are only two possible ways the boss can handle this. One is that the big boss is intimately knowledgeable about the business and understands the complete impact of each of these business escalations he or she is now managing. The other is that the big boss refuses to get involved and forces the "team" to manage the situation. The only practical solution is the latter, but it also requires a foundation to work properly.

In my humble opinion, solving the escalation culture problem mainly comes down to competence and trust. The "team" needs to demonstrate it has the competence to do the work and make the right decisions, and the big boss needs to trust the team to get on with things. Going halfway leads to chaos; unfortunately, this suits many people because it's easy to hide in chaos and, for the alert or the devious, there is much to be gained from chaos.

As a manager, it's mission-critical for you to find ways to handle customers' propensity to escalate, and to better manage your business.

When things are escalated *to* you, the first thing you need to do is pause. The second is to pause again. Before you get involved and enable the chaos, weigh the given request against the total business demands. If you get involved, you will undermine the people who should be taking care of the situation, even if they are the ones escalating it to you. If you have confidence in your managers and they have a proven track record of showing that they are capable of making sound business decisions, then trust them. If you do not trust your managers, then you will have to dig in and start micro-managing the situation. Once you are in this far, do not make the mistake of just solving the immediate problem. You must now address the larger issue of not trusting your key people to do the job they are responsible for doing. This means you must follow up with a reorganization.

Yes.

You read that correctly.

You'll have to get rid of them, unless you really want to wash, rinse, and repeat—which would not look good to *your* boss or shareholders. There will be many cases when the demands on your business and your teams are well above and beyond the given capacity to deliver. Resisting the impulse to react to the loudest voice or squeakiest wheel can be the correct decision. But don't make the mistake of telling your people to take care of things while at the same time constraining them.

An escalation culture is a bad one and, if it is the norm in your workplace, then your organization is broken. Identify the core organizational problem, which might begin with acknowledging immoveable constraints and the need to prioritize the problems. The fix may be to ensure you have enough staff to cope with all possible demands, but this is usually too expensive. The fix may be setting realistic expectations up front. The fix may be changing the faces in the office and bringing in some people who don't consider escalation to be an effective management tool. But, the fix will most certainly include communicating business realities openly so everyone has the same expectations. Then you can effectively stop the out-of-control escalations.

Chapter 30: "Not Invented Here" Syndrome

Arrogance can be blinding.

I'm referring to a situation I have seen many times, in which people are not open to ideas that come from outside their own world and, therefore, they end up making bad decisions. It always amazes me that people can block out sources of ideas purely because they did not think of the ideas themselves. How is anyone so arrogant that they are unable to acknowledge that other people can have better ways to do things, or ways to improve what was a Version 1.0? If you do not look to include all the available information sources in decisions, then what are you good for? And, frankly, what the hell are you doing in a managerial or executive role? This type of arrogant behavior can go undetected very easily, so if you know that it is normal human behavior for some of your people, don't ignore it. Do something about it.

Most problems you will face are like re-runs of the old shows on television. The vast majority of them are similar, if not identical, to the problems faced daily across the world and throughout history. When you need solutions, whether organizational or technical, use your team's collective brain power to think of solutions, but also try to find out how others have solved the challenge in the past and determine whether those solutions could be adapted to the situation you face. But first, check your arrogance at the office door.

Now that you are enlightened, you must look for the people in your organization who resist help or who are not open to discussion with others. Weed them out of your organization, or at least reassign them to a role that doesn't require anything other than rote thinking. Feel free to erase their whiteboard, you can be guaranteed that the best solution is *not* on it. Then, bring in someone to quickly assess the problems the former occupant of the position was apparently working on and leave them to it.

A great book called *The Myth of Innovation* by Scott Berkun offers a few reasons why people do not allow themselves to listen to or look for solutions from outside their limited world view. They are:

- Ego and envy: I can't accept this because I didn't think of it.
- Pride and politics: This makes me look bad.
- Fear: I'm afraid of change.
- Sloth: I'm lazy, bored, and don't want to think or do more work.

- Security: I may lose something I don't want to lose.
- Greed: I can make money or build an empire if I reject this idea.
- Consistency: This violates my deeply held principles (no matter how absurd, outdated, or ridiculous they are).

The list practically sums up the first season's plotlines of *The Office*, doesn't it? Be diligent and, when you come across these ignorant fools, counter their behavior and continually bring in the outside world to remind your company and your employees it is there. It is easy to forget but, if you provide the example of the behavior you want, and do it again and again, it will become part of the culture.

People

Chapter 31: We Are Watching You

Managers, make sure you wear the correct tie and shoes every Tuesday, and that your Casual Friday attire isn't too casual. People watch the actions, habits, and patterns of those they report to, and do so in more detail than you can imagine. I learned this vividly and in a very flattering way at a company, when several people who worked for me in the engineering team came to the company Halloween party "dressed like Richard." Being a man of limited imagination, I apparently had made it a routine to wear black trousers and a white button-down shirt most days. So, the team of about 20 people—men and women—came dressed in black and white. When I entered the conference room, I was surprised and a bit puzzled. It took me a few seconds to realize what was going on. It really was flattering and everyone had a good laugh.

135

You would be amazed how the very people who appear disinterested in you know your every little habit and quirk, and have opinions about them. If you diverge from what they perceive as your norm, some people see doom and gloom. I still am not sure why people are so enthralled by such things, but you might as well interpret it as a healthy fascination. Maybe they think that their fate is connected with yours.

Every email will have its critics, too, so you need to spend some time making sure they are well-structured and, at a minimum, factually correct. That being said, get on with it and send it already. Most of the audience will understand the message and take it at face value, even if there are a few small ambiguities or even errors in it. When you get stupid feedback — and you will — tell your critics it is stupid and move on.

The greatest opportunity for those in leadership positions is that you get to lead by example. If your example is worthy of positive imitation, then you have just found another tool to help make things better and improve the company's culture and its employees' lot in work. (Not "in life," which is a different thing, as noted earlier.)

If leading by example sounds like an alien concept, here are a few basics. Be polite to people, be respectful, and be seen. Make sure you walk around every day, if you can (and if you can't, then try harder). Take the risk of being misinterpreted by a few, so that you can get the message out to the 95 percent who will take your message and your means for what they are.

Chapter 32: Micro-Management: The Poster Child for Wasteful Management

Just say the term "micro-management" and someone's face springs to mind. Don't deny it. Every one of us has worked for or with someone who just couldn't *not* offer a comment, tweak a finished product, or find a flaw where none existed. I've often wondered what causes micro-management. Is it insecurity, is it a power issue, is it a lack of understanding, or is it a style of management? Micro-management is not as widespread as it could be, and that is a good thing. I see one or two in 10 managers who like to practice a ridiculous level of control. However, it cannot be emphasized enough that while only two in 10 managers would be classified as micro-managers, their negative effects on an organization can be substantial. If the micro-manager is at the top of the organization, then you will have a trickle-down effect and everyone is potentially involved.

If there is a situation in your organization that truly requires micro-management, this is a huge problem area for your business. You need to stop allowing it to be managed in this way and put in place people who can function independently and will accept responsibility for their actions and their outcomes. And you have to replace the micro-manager, who is usually the cause of problem. Of course, that won't be admitted to because he (or she) thinks everyone else is the problem. This won't come as a surprise because his actions indicate pretty clearly that his level of discernment and ability to perceive reality are clouded, at best.

The only really effective way out of the wasteful management environment is to change the micro-managers themselves, and I do not mean changing their ways through education. Get someone else in. If it is the CEO or company's owner, you may have to suffer a lot until the inevitable happens and the company goes bust or continues to underperform and never reaches its true potential and profitability.

Of course, there are masochists and robots out there who can take the pain of working for a micro-manager because of the insane pleasure suffering brings to them, or because of a healthy ability to completely ignore the reality in which they work and so go along with things and do as they are told. The second group may actually go home happy. No responsibility and they still get a paycheck — some people dream of jobs like that. If, however, you are relatively sane and mostly normal, leave

138

when you can. Go to another department. Go to another company. Just find a way out.

To the micro-manager (not that you know who you are): Give people responsibility and let them manage things. Hold them accountable. They can handle it.

People

Chapter 33: I Cannot Feel My Toes

Ya gotta love good old analysis paralysis.

You know how it works. There is an obvious decision that needs to be made. The question is clear. The choices are clear. Everyone thinks the answer is behind door Number One. But the person with the power or responsibility to open door Number One is asking detailed questions about the number of screws in the center hinge of door Number Four and it has not yet crossed his or her puny mind to turn the bloody knob. AHHHHH!

Don't despair. You have options.

The first option is to give in and stop pushing for a decision (see chapter on Passive Aggression). The second option is to reply that there are four screws in the hinge for door Number Four and then brace yourself for the next question, which will be along the lines of "Well, okay, if we look at the type–not number–of screws in the first two doors, taken as a set, and compare them to yesterday's lunch menu in the cafeteria — the set-course menu, not the *a la carte* menu — is there something in the comparison that needs to be considered before we move forward?"

AHHHHHHHHHHHHHHHHHHHH!

(See the chapters "The Perfect Boss" or "The Prefect Boss". Or maybe both.)

Do not get me wrong. Many, perhaps most, decisions would be better made after a good session of spirited dialogue with a bunch of clever people. They will raise things you simply forgot to include or did not understand to include. Perfect. But just because someone asks 'why?' five times in a row (the theory being that after five levels of 'why?' you will have uncovered the root cause) does not make them a management guru. Consider: every toddler on the planet does this.

So, don't perpetrate analysis paralysis or let yourself become a victim of someone else's. Be a grown-up. Take the available data and consider that timing can be crucial. Take some risks, but trust yourself and your team. But please, *please*, make a decision so that the rest of your team can get on with their work. Or face the following situation.

Having spent more than six weeks suffering with underperforming hardware, the siloed IT team was deep into its eighth meeting to determine the best course of action. There were people from the storage team, the applications team, the security team, the overall infrastructure team, the facilities team, and a sprinkling of managers and executives. Any question raised with more than 10 words in it seemed to take three individuals to answer, and most of the time they only could answer partially. This was going nowhere, slowly. Then, under the radar, someone who was living with the consequences of the poorly performing system, someone who was feeling the daily pain, decided to just drop-ship a new set of hardware and overnight switched out the old equipment with the new. By 6 a.m., it was ready to rock. The problem was solved by this enterprising individual—someone who had taken action.

However, the ninth meeting was not about celebrating the success of the transplant, it was about how it was possible that this individual had circumvented "the committee" and how many rules he or she may have broken. It reminded me of a very funny Monty Python scene in which the leaders of the People's Front of Judea sat around a table agreeing on the need for immediate action after their fellow rebel had been taken away by the Romans. They sat and talked and talked and sat, nodding in agreement about taking action but not actually taking any. In the end, there was lots of talk and no action. Think things through but in the end, and sooner than later, take action. Please.

People

Chapter 34: Power Loss (The Winter of Your Discontent)

It is the middle of winter and the holidays are upon you. You marvel at the first snowfall—so lovely, so peaceful, like sparkling fairy dust drifting down from heaven. Twelve hours later, you are staring out at the raging case of satanic dandruff that is obliterating everything from view. And then, just as you're about to go to sleep and hope it's all melted by morning, the power goes out and you are in a pitch-black house wondering where the flashlights are, and then where the batteries are. You look out the front window and wonder why the hell you aren't better friends with the neighbor whose generator, which sounds like a fleet of 747s at full throttle, will likely keep you up all night. You'll be freezing your ass off in the dark, possibly for days, and he'll be playing *Mortal Kombat* in comfort. For as long as he wants to.

Wait a minute.

What are all the other neighbors doing heading over — is that bastard having a blackout party? To which you would have been invited had you not demanded last May that his rubbish bin be taken off the street within two hours of the rubbish pickup and not left out until the next day because it was unsightly. (Yes, you actually said "unsightly.") You just had to say something. And this is the payoff.

Anyway, I digress.

In the workplace, power loss can be an equally strange and disconcerting occurrence, but significantly harder to bear because it can be a permanent thing. You were responsible for those three groups and now you have two. You can wonder why it was taken away, but you probably already know the answer. Chances are it was because the job was not getting the attention from you that it needed. While you may interpret this as a negative thing, it can also be that the company now needs more from that third group and no one can really do it part-time. Or that your other two groups are about to expand and you'll need the time for them.

If it happens to you, don't start bitching about the rubbish bins. Be a grown-up and accept what you probably cannot change. Try to understand the decision, and ask people, specifically your boss, why it was a necessary change. If you can keep your ego in check, you may be able to see that the changes are best for the company and, therefore, also best for you. The next thing — the very next thing — that you need to do is to get on board with the next person who is put in charge of your

146

former group. They will appreciate the help and, if you deal with the situation with maturity and grace, he or she will be a great ally later. Work with the new person, provide, or at least offer, support, and do what you can to foster the group's success. It will greatly increase your chances of getting invited to the next blackout party.

People

Part IV – The Actions

People

Chapter 35: Dealing with Things

You are very glad the day is over. It started inauspiciously when you discovered the open tin of paint in the boot of your car; it had been there for about a week and, like bad news, had spread itself everywhere. And, yes it was pink. Then that joke you made turned out to be insensitive and you annoyed someone you highly respect. The superstitious types among your peer group would say crap comes in threes, and number three was the news that a key part of your banner project is impossible and delays are inevitable.

None of these situations will improve with time. Most people would agree that it is easier to clean up a mess sooner rather than later.

Left unattended, the situation will not only not get better, it usually gets worse. The longer you procrastinate starting something, whether a project or a conversation, the harder it is to begin to deal with it. You could do what most people do, which is spend a lot of time asking their spouse/mother/therapist/hair stylist/pet ferret what they should do because they're stuck, paralyzed, embarrassed, hiding, or out of ideas. What they—and you—really are is afraid. People won't take the first step because it requires that they admit first a failure, a mistake. It can be a bit embarrassing and people are hesitant to lose face, especially at work, where you don't know what the ramifications might be.

Well, I am sorry for your troubles, but responsibility in business is for grown-ups. Taking responsibility and taking action are some of the things you're paid to do, so you just need to take the plunge. Keep track of your decisions, if you need to, and you will learn for yourself that the sooner you address an issue, the less worried you will be and that addressing things head-on will begin to get easier. Hopefully, you're the only one living inside your head and, therefore, only you can know what's blocking you from taking action. I'll leave the dilemma-sorting to you, but whatever the conclusion to that is *take action*. Truly, the easiest thing to do is simply to *act*. Do something and do it now. Make the call, schedule the meeting, change what needs to change, fix the problem.

Yes, doing that the first time requires a lot of self-control and a modicum of discipline. However, you will be happier working on a solution than festering over a problem, even if the actions for the solution are painful. The steps are simple:

- Make a list of the tasks that need your attention and action.
- Describe each task, assign it an owner, and set a target date for completion.

152

Whether or not you believe it, that was the hard bit and you have already done what most people cannot. Now, enter phase two:

- Talk to whomever you need to.
- Make it clear what the issue is.
- Ask for all the help you need.

Just make sure you are clear about what you or your team will do *personally* to fix things.

So that's the process for addressing project or organizational messes. When dealing with interpersonal conflicts, you need to approach them with the same sense of purpose, but with a slightly different methodology. These are situations with a face; therefore, you need to face them — literally — because it is what people deserve. It may be a bit uncomfortable, but that eases with practice. If they are good people, they will be adult enough to handle the conversation. If they are not adult enough, then they need a face-to-face to teach them a lesson or two about manners or humility, as the situation requires.

Dealing with stupidity is more troublesome. A lot of the time, the people do not know they are stupid. Sometimes, they are just playing dumb, which is worse. You will need to decide if your subject can be cured or whether your company can afford the luxury of paying someone who will never improve performance. But, you still have to act because, if you wait, the situation will be more out of control and will become even harder to fix.

Something that can help keep you organized and enable you to forecast trouble is an issue list. Modern workplaces have so many things happening on a daily basis that, in order to swim rather than sink, you must find a way to remind yourself of the tasks that need your attention. Keeping a list increases your odds of achieving greater success. Consider the list as a necessary tool. The results of using such a tool speak for themselves. It will give you a great feeling when things drop off the list because you addressed them.

By the way, do not put anything on your list that does not need to be there. You and everyone in your organization has a capacity limit for dealing with things, and the minute you have to deal with too many things, you will end up dealing with too few and doing them badly.

Chapter 36: Taking Back Time

As a manager, you no doubt live in a world where inadvertent time travel appears to be a reality. You start your day with a plan of action and optimistically begin work after that first cup of coffee or tea; then suddenly it is 3 p.m., it is 10 years later, your children are in college, and your hair has gone grey and has started to grow out of some startling places. WHAT HAPPENED? I will share some tips on how to regain control of your time and some rather large time sinks that you can avoid.

It is said that you should not put off until tomorrow what needs to be done today. And, just as importantly, consider putting off to *never* everything you can put off to three months from now because, if you can put it off that long, then maybe it is not worth doing at all.

Is that good advice or just some bluster?

155

Okay, I concede that strategic actions or initiatives will have a time horizon longer than three months by design and should not be dropped. Also, remember that inaction can be a real cost-saver and can definitely reduce the mistakes you can make.

Even when thinking in strategic terms, in most cases, it is not worth your time considering a time horizon longer than 18 months. This applies even more so to publicly-traded companies. You know, as do those pushing the initiatives, that the corporate reorganization cycle is reducing each decade and is now hovering around 18 months. You will rarely be measured on anything that far out. "You ignorant fool!" I hear you shouting, "What about companies with decades- or century-long histories?" Good question. How could they have managed to prosper without a long-term strategic view? Granted some did manage to create and maintain a coherent longer-term strategy but many more set a strategy and changed it again and again as their world changed.

You have limited time available during your work life, so you must pick the right tasks and the right time horizon so you can be most effective. Do the right things for the right reasons and find ways to rationalize the multitude of demands you can handle or paths you can take. Even more important than doing the right things—and more difficult things—is not to waste your time doing tasks that have no value.

Focus most of your attention on the tactical and near-term targets, by which I mean three months or less. If you focus on these, get them done well, and get on with the next set, you will accumulate many successes which will deliver longer term positive outcomes.

People

Chapter 37: Sharing the Love – Not So Much, Please

How much should you bring a customer into your processes? It depends on whether you have a lot of time on your hands and nothing better with which to fill it. I do not think you should open up too much, because this newfound "knowledge" on the part of the customer will inevitably be accompanied by opinions, which will be followed by suggestions and the expectation that you will implement them. After all, the customer will think you have brought them into the equation. And you will be left to weakly explain that they are not in the equation, you were just trying to make friends with them, impress them, or something else equally stupid. Instead, define goals and criteria that are real things the customers will be able to use to see progress, and then use these and *only* these when reporting status to your customers. This keeps emotion out of it and reduces too much interference.

Managing the customer relationship at arm's length is also a good internal defensive move because it will save you from those people who use the customer as leverage for their own agenda. An example is when a sales person feeds the customer a question or demand that the customer then uses as their own. The customer suddenly approaches you with a strong "suggestion" that at a minimum will eat up time and effort to investigate and argue, even though it was probably already taken off the table internally. Do not allow the customer relationship to be used as a weapon by anyone in your company. Putting unnecessary pressure on the team won't necessarily pay off, but bringing the customer into the process redefines the customer relationship and, once that happens, there is no going back to the way things used to be.

In my experience, there are two perspectives when it comes to bringing the customer in, and each perspective is guided by the degree of the relationship with the customer. Sales, which wants to nurture the relationship, wants more involvement. Those who perform the task the customer needs the company to deliver — engineering, manufacturing, etc. — will have a different perspective. All sides need to understand that distraction from the mission leads to trouble. Your people's performance will suffer, which means the product or schedule could suffer, which would lead to customer dissatisfaction.

That is not to pretend that any company or team can fully control the situation, so at times the customer will be more closely involved than you prefer. You need to make the most and the least of these circumstances. Get what you can from the interaction, but keep it as brief and on-topic as possible.

The last word on the topic is to remember that you will have oodles of time that needs to be spent with the customer when you deliver the product or service.

People

Chapter 38: Communications

As you can probably tell from trying to interpret this book, communication is not a simple task. You get ideas, you think you are being clear, but still end up with unsatisfying results. There are some simple pitfalls that you can avoid and, once you master that skill, you can concentrate on honing the actual messages you communicate.

Solution to Pitfall #1: The Emotional Email. I know you have experienced pressure at work that at times may cloud your judgement or cause you to overreact or misinterpret things. One such situation that we strongly react to is the perception or realization that you are being slighted, particularly via email because you never know who else will see it. Because we're all human, or close to it, things will get emotional at times, but you should never respond to emotional emails with emotional emails.

Let me repeat that: you should never respond to emotional emails with emotional emails.

That way lies madness, at best, and career implosion, at worst. By all means, go ahead and write down your response, but make sure to take the name or names out of the *To* field so that you can't inadvertently send it. Save it as a draft, if you must, but think twice before hitting Send. You can never get it back and, inevitably, you will regret having sent it and will not be happy with the consequences of having sent it. This is not to say that you must let the original sender of the first email get away with bad behavior, but you must exorcise your inner adolescent and respond as an adult.

An example of how to handle this happened not too long ago in an organization I was involved with. There were two female colleagues who routinely butted heads, which is a different issue. One — Ann — sent an email to the other — Sue — asking for information. It was a polite, non-inciting email, and the response was more or less the same. Except that the *To* line on the response included the original sender's name (Ann) and the additional words "The Cow." And the sender of the second email (Sue) had included four additional people on the email. Ann responded to the content of the second email in a businesslike manner but, at the end of the email, politely asked Sue to explain herself. Sue explained that she'd put that addition in her contact list in a fit of annoyance.

Unfortunately for her, that one moment of childish satisfaction left a permanent, damning paper trail of her inability to handle situations

164

appropriately and created an unforgettable impression in the minds of all the recipients—and to whomever they might have forwarded it. So, please, think long and hard before hitting Send when your emotions are in the driver's seat.

Solution to Pitfall #2: Don't "disappoint." What I mean here is that you should delete all variations of the term "disappoint" from your business vocabulary. It invariably inspires a negative reaction in the recipient. Anyone who has been a parent in the last 40 years knows that this term is touted as one of the best for conveying displeasure and instilling shame when children misbehave. That is not the appropriate relationship for a work environment, despite the natural hierarchies that exist. Shaming a peer or subordinate is going to create an obstacle in the relationship that will be difficult, if not impossible, to overcome and will clearly establish you as a charter member of the assholes club.

Solution to Pitfall #3: Cancellation Revelation. To the degree that it's possible, never cancel a meeting with a customer or one of the people you manage because of a meeting your boss has scheduled over you. Easy for me to say, right? I hear your protest, but this is very important for the following reason: the ability to establish and honor your priorities is a key element of success. Your boss should understand this.

Solution to Pitfall #4: R-E-S-P-E-C-T—Find out what it means to *them*. Communication in meetings must be considered and executed carefully because the impact of face-to-face interaction is greater than the impact of written communication, which is more impersonal. You must make sure that meetings remain respectful and that people are

165

comfortable enough to participate and contribute. Don't shy away from accountability; if someone has failed to do an assigned task, you have to bring it up. Ask about the failure and ask about how it's going to be remedied or resolved. Just make sure you do it in a clear and respectful way. Most people in the room will already be aware of the failure, and the person responsible will probably be expecting you to bring it up. So, not asking about it may well end up making you look weak or hesitant, and neither of those attributes will gain you the respect you need from your employees to do your job well.

Solution to Pitfall #5: Relying on email when a conversation will do. Email is great, except when you need to convey information that has some emotional or ambiguous aspect to it, or information that could be misinterpreted. People need to talk with people and doing so will greatly reduce the misunderstandings that trap us in awkward situations. Face-to-face is best, but a phone call is a good second choice.

Solution to Pitfall #6: What part of "Do this" did you not understand? I admit to being perplexed when, after an inspired speech or discussion that was clearly a call to action, people have not done what I expected them to do. Sometimes, they have not even begun to do what I've asked them to do after having asked several times. Before I take any drastic steps—firing them, reassigning them, or even just having a come-to-Jesus meeting with them—I stop to check if I am the point of failure in the communication path. I review the situation to determine if I've been clear about my expectations. I ask myself if I was asking them to do something they saw as a waste of time. Then, I ask them the same

166

questions. Such discussions can be eye-opening. And it's not always them. Sometimes, it's just that my delivery was flawed or lacking in some critical element, such as the appropriate sense of urgency or expectation. Improve your effectiveness when communicating with others by being self-critical after unsuccessful attempts. And be prepared for surprises and to learn somethings that you can personally improve.

Solution to Pitfall #7: Let the people speak. Sharing information is critical, but you don't always have to be the source. I've found that a good technique is to make the people actively involved in the situation be the source, especially if it's good news. It makes a big difference to people, and allows them to see the effects of their own words. If they are sharing experiences, success or otherwise, it is more powerful than if the big boss just summarizes what everyone has been doing. So often, those summaries focus on the big issues, such as profit and loss or a big sale, and lose the details that can mean a lot to the people involved, such as how they overcame specific challenges they faced or how they came up with the tactic they used to beat the competitor.

There are a lot of hawks in my neighborhood, and they always let us know loud and clear when they're on the hunt by sending piercing cries to each other from their perches on the rooftops. As majestic and fierce as they are, it's satisfying to see one or even more of them chased out of the area by a single mockingbird that is a third their size. So, get others in the management chain to be regular communicators and let the smaller birds flap their wings sometimes. You might be impressed with the results, and your employees will certainly appreciate the opportunity to share.

Solution to Pitfall #8: Don't nobody bring me no bad news. Delivering hard news is an especially tough part of the job and it's a constant, right up there with death and taxes. Everyone knows that businesses have many ups and downs over the course of their lifespan. As a manager, you need to be mature and deal with both the ups and especially the downs directly, efficiently, and with humanity. I've had to deliver a lot of bad news in the course of my career, more with each step up the ladder, but I am routinely amazed at people's reactions. More often than not, the reaction is calm acceptance, although sometimes that calm is buttressed by a bit of shock. People understand that there are valid reasons for bad news, even when it affects them personally, and can usually handle it when it is presented accurately and with an appropriate amount of compassion. There was only one time in my experience when a person really couldn't handle the stress of *potentially* hearing bad news, but that had more to do with the person than the news.

The situation was a performance review of a relatively new middle manager who knew he wasn't performing well, yet wouldn't make the changes we'd asked him to make. Before the review even started — before I even walked into his office — he was retching into his wastebasket and sweating profusely. By the time I walked in, I was wondering if he was having a heart attack. At his explanation that he doesn't handle stress well (understatement of the century), I offered to conduct the review at a later time. He refused, and just kept sweating and retching. Needless to say, it was a quick discussion. Later in the day, he ended up heading to the ER with chest pains. The whole circumstance was bizarre, and certainly unnerving for both of us. (He was fine, by the way.)

Granted, that situation was extreme and unexpected, but he got through it. Had that been conducted over the telephone, I don't know how it might have turned out, but it reinforces that the face-to-face approach is the best in many circumstances, with a personal phone call the second best. Email is not the way to deliver bad news unless you need to get the message out to people in different locations at the same moment and a conference call or web call is not an option. However, you need to deliver the news: do it quickly, calmly, compassionately, and get it over with, or it will fester and grow in your brain—and possibly the recipient's gut.

People

Part V – Corporate Movements

People

Chapter 39: Reorganize, Renew, Repeat (The Three Rs)

Many times, people look at corporate reorganizations as negative events that must be rallied against. It takes some experience to understand the circle-of-life in the corporate world; it is very cyclical. After some time, you also will learn that fighting the natural cycle of reorganizations is not the best thing to do. The discussion about an impending reorganization should never be framed as good versus bad, fighting back the tide, or winning and losing. People use these terms quite often, but I contend that using your energies to fight these changes is wasteful and will only frustrate you because, in most cases, you will not have control over the process or the plan. The better approach is to learn that the routine of reorganize, renew, and repeat is a normal part of business these days and, to a lesser extent, a normal part of life.

173

You are familiar with what are called "life-events," such as getting married, buying your first house, getting divorced, moving back in with your parents. Some are good and some are bad, but we are expected to take them in stride because they are part of the normal flow of things. It is the same in corporate life. There are types of corporate events, such as reorganizations and staff ramp-ups or reductions, that are just part of the normal flow of business, with some more pleasant than others and some that are contrived and wasteful.

How you handle these corporate events is a matter of choice. You can fight, flee, hide, or cry, or deal with it some other way. To make the right choice, you need to understand the reasoning behind the corporate decision and its context in the wider culture of the organization. If you believe the decision/event is good for the company (or maybe just for yourself), either in the long run or the short run, then work with it and make the most of it. If you believe it is just a cynical attempt to avoid fixing real problems by launching another reorganization, then you probably do not plan to be enthusiastic. In the latter case, carefully consider what you will do because, clearly, someone in the company is driving the event and believes in it. You don't want to put yourself in an awkward position with a higher power, if you can avoid it.

Here are a few important reasons why companies undertake reorganize or renewal:

- The company/division is losing money and something dramatic needs to be done to stop the hemorrhaging.
- Power has changed hands and the new person in charge wants things to be done differently.

174

- A great innovative opportunity has arisen and the business needs to be in a different form to successfully compete and win.

Depending on how often the organization engages in this behavior, there will be people who have been around for a long time and will have seen these cycles come and go. These long-term employees may even recognize the plan being presented because it may be identical to a plan that was attempted in the past, unsuccessfully. If you are part of this group, you need to think carefully about what to do and how you should react to the latest round of changes. Acting jaded, obstructive, or — worse — self-righteous, will do you no good, so don't attempt it. Don't even *consider* attempting it. If you do not want to participate, feel free to leave. However, I would advise you to help — really help. Don't just go through the motions. That's passive-aggressive and will be noticed by more people than you might think would notice.

I sat through the initial presentation of one such reorganization at a company. I was part of the leadership team and participated in structuring the reorganization and understood the drivers well. It was also well known that something similar had been attempted about 10 years prior and had only partially worked. True to form, one member of the old guard took the opportunity during the Q-and-A session to declare his disbelief that the company was going to try this folly yet again. He related anecdotes, expounded on the many hurdles that stopped the earlier effort, and listed many reasons why the new plan just did not fit the company culture. We all listened and when his bag of obstructions was fully deflated, the CEO took the opportunity to respond. His response was simply to say that the goals for the company

175

were very clear and simple and the only thing that was needed from the team was to apply their positive energy to making the company, their teams, and themselves better. The CEO neatly and completely took apart each argument presented and it became clear that the manager objecting to the new effort was probably one of the people responsible for the failure of the improvement efforts in the past.

So, shake off the past, but do not forget it. Now that you are wiser and know the company better, see what new things you can do to help the plan succeed this time. That, too, will be noticed.

Whatever the reasons behind your organization's Three Rs (Reorganize, Renew, Repeat), make an effort to find your peace with them because, in business, these activities are necessary for the success of the business and for the success of individuals. You and your team can take advantage, in a good way, of the opportunities the changes will present and you might gain valuable experience, a new position, a higher profile, or additional responsibility because of them.

Chapter 40: Downsizing

Downsizing is a situation unto itself in the corporate world, and I'm differentiating it from the many and varied issues that would be covered by the advice in the previous chapter. The one thing that is true across the board is that, just like handling other changes, handling downsizing in a company is very tough. It is rarely a great experience and the whole affair is usually a pain in the neck, especially if you are part of the downsized group. However, there are sensible ways to manage it successfully and treat people well.

If you find yourself one of a group of managers who have been instructed to contribute to a downsizing, do not assume the other managers will comply with the instructions or will be willing to give up money or people in a fair-handed way. Being the first to move and offer up bodies or budgets in a situation like this is not the best course of action.

When you are directed to take the drastic measure of downsizing, you should fight the reductions, force the issue, and question both the reasoning and evidence in detail. You must do this to satisfy yourself that removing people from their jobs and their income is the right action for the company. Take a hard, realistic look at the situation and ask the tough questions. Determine for yourself whether the business environment has changed so much that there is not enough work to keep people busy or not enough revenue to support the cost base. Find out if the company has exited some area and no longer needs the people who supported it, and if there is a way to redeploy them. Ask the people who made the decision if downsizing will put the company in a better position financially and, therefore, ensure that the rest of the staff is unlikely to be dismissed at some near-future date. It is your responsibility to understand as much as you can about the situation because you will be asked about these issues by your staff, and the people who will be most affected by the cuts deserve some respect from you and some rationale for the corporate decisions.

If it ends up, as it often does, that you will still have to downsize, one technique I have seen work in the past is very simple and involves patience and a thick skin: do not offer up anything or anyone for as long as you can get away with it.

Instead, in meeting after meeting, state your case that you cannot do without the team you have, but make sure your argument is based on the truth. Your fellow managers and your boss will get irritated with you, for sure. However, if there is a weaker member of your peer group, that person may get lazy or tired of waiting, and offer more from their team just to move things along. Of course, you could very well decide to take the latter way out of the situation, but I'll state right now that I think doing that is ridiculous. I consider it scandalous that any manager could care so little for his or her team that impatience would be the driving force to put people out of work, even though I have seen it work.

When it is finally time to face the music and review the downsizing options, be ready. There is nothing stronger than clear reasoning. Bring facts and figures to the discussion, and talk about the real impacts on work and customers. Topics for discussion should include the ramifications of a smaller staff on how certain tasks are to be completed — or not — and how to handle customer requests. It is most important to be logical and to support your arguments clearly. If you insist on coming to such a discussion unprepared and without clear data to support all eventualities, then you are a coward and should leave the company; the people working for you deserve more respect.

When the time comes, you must be realistic and fair in your decisions. If economic circumstances and your analysis of the situation dictate that downsizing is unavoidable, then apply yourself. Eliminate the position and the corresponding work, or redistribute it.

Telling people that they no longer have a job is never a pleasant task but, as bad as it is for you to deliver the news, the situation is significantly more unpleasant for the people who lose their jobs.

Concentrate on making the experience as respectful as possible and do what you can to be generous, so that those losing their jobs have a little help for when they start their search for their next one.

After the downsizing has been implemented, you must adjust to your new situation. You will be able to get along without the staff, but expect things to be bumpy.

Chapter 41: Upsizing

Hurray, business is booming, your company has won a lot of new business, and the challenge to deliver has been placed on your desk. You are a great manager and your current team is working well and efficiently, you are confident that you will need more people to meet the challenge of the new business. As a manager, you will need to make sure you can clearly justify the extra people and be ready to argue the case to whomever controls the budget.

Now it is time to find those needed people, time to start the dreaded interviewing dance. There are some great people out there and you need to find ways of attracting them and choosing them. In most cases, you will have many more candidates apply for the jobs you have than there are jobs. On occasion, you might end up with more than one "perfect" candidate for a position. More often, you will not find Mr. or Ms. Perfect

181

and will have to take a risk on a candidate you think could do the job well. Keep in mind that your decision is based on evidence that is normally circumstantial: the résumé, the references, and the interview.

You will have to contact candidates' references, so make sure you have a large pinch of salt nearby when you do so. It's highly unlikely that someone looking for a job could be so clueless as to point you to a dud who may say something bad about them. Expect high praise and ask tough questions that require more than a yes or no. Often, the length of the reference's hesitation before answering a question can reveal more than the answer that's eventually given. Ditto for the responses from the candidate, but references have a different horse in the race than a candidate does, so construct your questions accordingly and listen to the answers with a different filter.

The actual face-to-face interview is typically the most nerve-wracking part of the process, but it doesn't have to be. You know that the candidate will be nervous — unless you get the over-confident, cocky sort, who is just a pain in the ass for everyone. Irrespective of what sort of candidate walks into your office for the interview, your first impression will dictate a lot of what happens in the interview. Trust your gut, but don't let it override your brain. Everyone knows about body language — if you don't, there are enough books and TED talks on the subject to keep you in slack-jawed hibernation for a few weeks. Just keep in mind that people are individuals and have their idiosyncrasies and, when people are nervous, they may not behave as they normally would.

Despite the effect that being in the situation can have on people, I have found that when I've asked interviewees direct questions about what they are good or bad at or, better yet, what annoys them or pushes their buttons, I get what seem to be honest answers, even if they are negative. I'm frequently quite surprised by it. One candidate I interviewed came across as a very pleasant level-headed person. He had the right skills and an impressive breadth of experience. I asked one of my standard questions: "What annoys you?" We are all human and there is always something that would annoy us, so I ask upfront and usually get an honest answer. In this case, I was amazed that he said "When people question me, I get annoyed. They should just trust me and not challenge me." Well, he got a point for honesty. But, we all need to be challenged; it is part of a healthy organization to have constructive challenges happening all the time. Needless to say, I did not hire this time-bomb.

A manager needs to trust his or her instincts when hiring and, if there are doubts in your mind, pay attention to them. Just know that you will make a bad choice every now and then, and will be utterly surprised by what the "genius" you hired does; just act as quickly as you can and replace the person, if that's what's necessary.

In my experience, the safest route for making a hiring decision is to go for consensus. Go ahead and re-read that sentence if you need to. It's not a typo—I actually do think full consensus is possible, perhaps even probable. I also think it's the safest and most logical bet, and a result that you should seek out. If you have had several people interview a

183

candidate and even one of the interviewers expresses well thought-out concerns or doubts, listen — especially if you trust that person's opinion. Discuss the concerns as a group, or at least get everyone's input. If consensus cannot be reached, you should consider waiting for another candidate who appeals to all. Let me also be clear that you should only include interviewers who do not have their own agenda, for instance someone who may feel threatened by the candidate.

Remember that no organizational structure is sacred. When you get the opportunity to grow, take a hard look at the structure. Change, to the degree you're able, everything you think needs to be changed, and do it as soon as you have decided on the alternative.

Being in a growth environment affects the collective mood of the employees in a good way. It is people who are crucial to growth so, when hiring, set your standards very high, trust the consensus opinion (in most cases), and accept that, without first-hand experience of the prospective candidate, you can never be entirely sure how well he or she will work out. Trust your judgment and correct any mistakes you make in the hiring as early as you can.

Chapter 42: Motivating People – Helping to Drive Performance

Figuring out the best way to motivate people is a very tough puzzle. Many bright people have struggled to solve it with only partial success – and many have failed miserably. Ensuring that your employees do what you need them to do and ensuring that they believe their job is worthwhile aren't the biggest challenges a manager faces, but they are consistent ones. There is no a simple solution.

It takes a concerted effort to get *and keep* people motivated. The secret is to work out what is reasonable to ask of your employees and ensuring that, with hard work, it will be possible for them to achieve the goals you set for them. You need to make certain the reward you are offering for achieving those goals is a genuine one. You must also consider the "jaded" factor and expect your oft-repeated push for them to "go the extra mile" to be greeted with decreasing enthusiasm. This is most likely not due to laziness. Rather, it is due to "enthusiasm fatigue." Think about it: Is it reasonable to assume people will get enthused *again* about the latest corporate initiative after being asked to get revved up for the last several dozen? People need a break between these "big" pushes or drives and, by the way, care should be taken to ensure the initiatives really are "big" or important. It's no different than engaging in any other strenuous exercise; people need to rest between bouts or they will wear out and their performance will drop to nothing.

It's not enough to devise a great corporate strategy with clear goals and communicate this glorious plan to your people with the expectation that you will convince enough of them on the first go to start executing your plan successfully. Experience has shown me that a lot of companies fail to meet their goals, and most actually miss by a long way. The reasons are many but, typically, highest on the list are a lack of a shared understanding and no real buy-in. Put bluntly, the employees were not convinced. If you want your company to be a member of the small group with a positive outcome, ask these questions during the planning process:

- Are the goals realistic and achievable?
- What amount of time and human effort will it take to meet the goals?
- Can you convince the management and staff that the plan is worthwhile?
- Is the "reward" you are offering just "survival," with the underlying message that, if the plan fails, jobs will be lost??
- Does your plan to persuade people include bullying?

People

The people working for you and those leading your company will include many smart people on whom you are going to rely to help reach the company's targets. Don't insult their intelligence by trying to tell them the road will be short and fast if you know it will be neither. People do not forget how they are treated, and nobody responds well to being threatened, no matter if it's just implied. Be able to show them how the goals can be achieved and make sure your argument is clear and convincing. To convince people, it is best to know what you are talking about and to be truthful. *You* need to honestly believe that achieving the goals is possible and that you have at least one path that could work. Don't imply that your goals are easy—you have to be the dreamer—but they had better be doable. That is the secret to motivating people.

There is a huge body of work available on motivation and demotivation, so please do yourself and your teams a great service and spend time researching and studying the many human factors in motivation.

People

Chapter 43: Change Agents – Ha! Ha!

Let's dissect the term "change agents." In the jargon of the moment, it identifies the people whose job it is to direct and manage change. Since when did this role slip away from, oh, everyone in the management structure of the company? Seriously, does a company need a separate tier on the org chart for this? Fire or reassign the bloody change agents! The job of directing and managing change belongs to the people charged with implementing the company vision and strategy — in other words, you and everyone else above and below you. Managers need to take the visions and strategy and do whatever is needed to achieve them, including making changes, when warranted.

And *please* stop saying nonsensical things like "things change" and "we need to embrace change." These are tired, overused statements that are guaranteed to trigger a negative reaction in an almost Pavlovian

189

way. Grown-ups understand grown-up language, so just tell it to them straight: our products are not selling as well as they used to and something needs to be done to address this. Then identify the "something," whether it's reducing costs, adding a feature customers have asked for, but has not been provided, or whatever else the solution might be.

I imagine that most of the people who work for you are not mindless idiots and, therefore, they are not going to respond well to corporate bullshit in the abstract. Change happens all the time, so you don't need a dedicated staff to "manage" it. You'll be better off hiring some administrative assistants to increase the efficiency of your other staff while they do their jobs, which includes, just by the way, managing change.

Enough said.

Chapter 44: A Company That is a Good Social Partner

Make sure that your company gets involved in the local community, whether by engaging in some charity or civic work, or other projects. Helping others is a good thing to do and it feels so right that it should be a natural and obvious undertaking. Just ask people in your company if they are willing to get involved. Most people are willing to give their time and effort to help a good cause. The company itself also needs to help, and one good way is to choose a non-political, non-religious, non-controversial cause to support and then encourage and allow employees the time to help out. Just make sure what you take on is a real cause that will provide real results to a population in need and be sure your company can deliver on its promises. Everyone who participates will get plenty of satisfaction out of it.

In one company I worked for, a small team of very generous people got together and organized a year-long campaign to raise money for local families in need. They organized breakfasts, birthday cakes, and ice cream lunches, all to raise a few dollars at a time for the cause. Then, just before Christmas each year, they would take the money raised and buy supplies and presents to give to the chosen families so that there would be presents under the tree for the children and some extra food and clothing for the holidays.

Apart from the tremendous effect this had on the families in the community, there was also a benefit to the employees who participated. The employees' reward was a sense of personal satisfaction and the knowledge that they helped real people in a very immediate and much—needed way; beyond that, the fundraising events allowed co-workers to enjoy some time together regularly to just say hello and chat.

I suggest that you don't make financial considerations your first qualifier and that you don't get involved in something just because it will make you or your company look good. Expecting some sort of financial or other benefit for your company hollows out the experience. Just do it to help out and to make a difference.

Another suggestion is to go local, where possible. There are many ways to go national or global, but your efforts will have a deeper effect on your people if you go local. They will be able to see and possibly participate in the results. The locals will appreciate it, too.

Chapter 45: Leading an Organization to Greatness

It can be very tempting to find a catchy and concise way to explain the vast subject of business success and many writers have taken it to extremes. Think about the book *Blink*, which basically says that you come up with great ideas in the blink of an eye and that if you follow through on that inspired thought then you will reach the top. In a word: bullshit; it is all about hard work.

I believe there is no shortcut for any company that wants to be on the top of the charts. In fact, there is nothing secret about what it takes to achieve greatness as a company. The main reason many companies fail to live up to their potential is that they look for a quick or easy solution when much of the time success will only come when you do the hard work and have world-class execution.

While I will not distill the process down to a blink of an eye, I will concentrate on what I think are the top three most important areas that will bring your company success, if you actually execute.

In reverse order of importance:

3. Spend Wisely. You must ensure that your company is investing its money and people resources in the right areas. This applies to many areas in which you must choose wisely what you will invest in to meet long-term plans. It also applies to how smart you work; in other words, ensure you are not wasting scarce resources on things that will not create the raving fans you need as customers for long-term success. Be a good steward of your resources and put in the hard work, study, and research to know that you are investing wisely for your customers' future and your own.

2. Continuously Improve Quality. You must ensure your company is finding ways to continuously improve the products and services you offer and the processes you use to create and deliver the same. This is necessary to retain your current customers and to be able to differentiate your company and pull ahead of your competition. Every area of your business will have numerous opportunities to improve and you should be on a never-ending campaign to identify those opportunities and deliver the improvements.

And finally,

1. Meet Your Commitments. To be a world-class company and be better than your competition, you must ensure that all your great plans and good intentions are realized. You need to state out loud what you plan to do and then 1) do it, 2) do it right, and 3) do it when you said you would. This applies to all of the internal goals within your company and to the commitments you make to your customers. When customers see that you are a reliable supplier or partner, one who makes and meets its commitments, then those customers will reward you with more business, directly and by recommending you to others.

So, remember, spend wisely, continuously improve quality and, most importantly, meet your commitments.

People

Chapter 46: A MADD Approach to Recovery in Stormy Times

The character of a company and its people is rarely tested during the highs. Certainly, when business is booming, there are many stresses. But, in good times, those stresses are missing an edge — the fear of failure and what it might mean for the company and its people. The true character of a company, its people, and its leaders comes to light when the lows happen. When a business is knocked back a step and needs to find the strength of character to soak it up and recover is the time for level-headed, realistic leaders who believe in the business and its future to step forward and lead the way. These are the times when sanity must prevail.

This is the point at which it's time to take *A MADD* approach to dealing with business recovery and improvement.

Avoid

The first step of A MADD approach is to *avoid* allowing issues to arise. Do whatever is needed to avoid the typical pitfalls, which are ignoring quality issues, ramping up too quickly without revenue backing, spending on product development that will not be profitable, shipping too early, etc. Unfortunately, the avoidance list is long and varied, and keeping a company on track day in and day out is the challenge you will constantly face. That's why it's important to look forward realistically while protecting your current place in the market.

Mobilize

When you have not successfully avoided a disruption, the company must *mobilize* toward recovery. Identify the people who are best suited to driving the company out of the current situation. Keep an open mind about whom you choose for the team: do not limit the team to the current leadership. Search inside and outside of your organization for the best people to get involved, and look at all levels in your company. Whomever you choose, do so carefully because you want people who are willing and able to help. You want people who will check their egos at the door, roll up their sleeves, and provide constructive and informed input.

Analyze

The next step is to buckle down and *analyze* the data and information using a cold, critical, objective eye. You must gather concrete evidence to define the situation, the issues, and the possible solutions. I advise taking some time with this step to avoid panicking or implementing a half-baked course of action; you will have plenty of time to make the business-risk decisions in the near future. Another must: remove the word "assume" from the conversation and replace it with some research and data. Granted, some of your analysis will come up short of a satisfactory level of detail or data, but you must resist settling for less-than-ideal information too soon. That could be what put you into the mess in the first place, so do the hard work to find out everything you can. It is also crucial to put a hard time limit on this phase, because timing is very important in these situations.

Decide

The next step is to *decide* on a course of action or, perhaps, more than one. When you have exhausted the avenues for research and analysis, or the reasonable timeframe you set is over, it is time to answer the question, "What are we going to do?" The worst answer is "Nothing. Let's see what happens." A close second is "Let's try to wait it out." The best answer is "We will do this one thing and we are 100% confident it will correct our situation." But no one ever says that with a straight face. In reality, you will answer, "We have identified X things (X being not more than five) and we have medium- to high-levels of confidence that the combination of actions will improve our situation."

199

Deliver.

Now, you must *deliver*. Bring the needed teams together and communicate the course of action. Spend time to get buy-in, but limit that time. You will need to move quickly to get the business back on course, and time is of the essence. So, consult in good faith and deliberate with key people, but be prepared to get started. Choose the path and MOVE, MOVE, MOVE!

Assign responsibilities and set targets publicly to help get everyone on the same page. In times of crisis or times when you need a change in mindset, going public with your decisions and goals and being visibly accountable is a very powerful tool.

Drive the changes to their intended conclusion while being prepared to adjust course if you encounter unexpected negative results. Execution is always the one thing that differentiates successful from unsuccessful programs. To execute effectively, you need people who believe in the path and are working day in and day out to remove barriers that prevent success.

By the way, feel free to deploy A MADD approach even when everything is running smoothly because these steps work just as well for ongoing improvements.

Chapter 47: How to Kick Start a Cultural Change

When I hear people talk self-righteously about a cultural problem in a company, a division, or a department, I am reminded of the many conversations I have witnessed in which someone is holding court about how bad drivers are in a particular country, state, or city. I have been lucky enough to live and work in many countries around the world and in many states in the USA. I have also travelled extensively and seen and been a part of the traffic adventures in Dublin on the Emerald Isle, Sydney in "The Land Down Under", along the by-roads around the Taj Mahal, on the roads from Beijing to the Great Wall of China, and in the dizzying madness encircling the Arc de Triomphe in Paris—at night.

201

I've come to believe it must be one of our ingrained human characteristics that we are very quick to make observations about how bad other people are at something, while being able to blithely ignore any shortcomings we may have ourselves. Too frequently, we take it even further and become self-proclaimed experts or poster children for how things should be or should be done, while everyone else deserves derision.

This is why we should use a mirror to help us get started on any improvement initiative. Look deep into the blue, green, brown, hazel or bloodshot eyes you see in the mirror and ask yourself what you can do to change this current reality. Take the same mirror and hold it up to your group and your company and ask the same question. Before any change can occur, you need to know what you are willing to change and whether you are willing to put in the tremendous effort it will take to make the change happen.

Kick-starting a cultural change is that simple. Look in the mirror and take an honest look—yes, an honest look—and start with what you see. Success in undertaking a cultural change will come from an unceasing drive by you, your team.

Part VI – Simple Stuff

People

Chapter 48: Slicing Things Up: *Where Did All My Free Time Go?*

I have come across many people who regard the problem of getting their work done in a timely fashion as their biggest challenge, or at least in their top three. Many books and articles address the seemingly modern problem of time management. They detail various strategies and techniques that will make your life manageable and feel like it is under control. These books do serve up 'simple' ways to take control, many of which include making a prioritized list and then starting at the top and working your way through until you have finished everything. Earth-shattering idea. In addition, there are a variety of treats offered to break the monotony and boredom of running your work life as a slave to a list. These are usually along the lines of another earth-shattering idea, such as finding something on or off the list that you find enjoyable

205

as a reward to yourself and then quickly getting back to the order you know you need follow.

It is a matter of fact that you will get loaded with as many things as you can handle, and then some. The expectation from your boss is rarely that you will get everything done as planned, but they need to have you deliver as much as you possibly can and earn your money. The boss expects you to be efficient and organized, so if you are overloaded because you are disorganized, then you have some improvements to work on. However, if it is because there are simply too many competing demands and if you truly cannot find a solution, then go to your boss and explain the situation clearly. Ask him or her to set your priorities or to leave some tasks unassigned, delayed, or assigned to someone else.

In the modern world, with its single-minded orientation toward the combination of high profits and high productivity, you find yourself in a constant struggle facing more requests than are "reasonable" for any one person to satisfy. Prioritizing is critical to success. Determine who you need to talk to about priorities—the boss, the customer, your peers—and then open the discussion. Find out what is *really* needed to complete the project—not the 'would be nice' parts, but the truly necessary parts—and then find out how those things need to be prioritized. Figure out if you have enough time or people to deliver it. If not, get more time or more people, then get started and don't stop until you're finished. Yes, these are tough conversations. Have them anyway.

Do not be lazy. Know that it is expected you are working hard most of the time and very hard every so often. Get yourself organized and plan your work and be open to sharing the challenges with others, rather than letting things slide. When there are clear expectations about a report being delivered on time or the customer product shipping as promised, don't make disappointment be the default no-action result. Raise the issue and deal with it *now*. In essence, act like an adult and do not hide bad news; it will be better received before the event than after.

The reality of managerial multi-tasking will not go away and it takes time to adjust to it, but you need to get a grip on it, keep a list, and prioritize it, otherwise the constant pressure in a situation of hard constraints will drive you nuts. With a sustained effort, you will succeed in taming it.

So, remember, keep it simple and,

1) Make a list.
2) Prioritize the list and re-prioritize as needed. However, you must try very hard to avoid doing the latter for tasks already started, because it will cause disruption and loss of momentum, both of which lead to wasted effort and time and lower morale.
3) Start at the top and work your way through the list until you have finished everything you needed to do.
4) Take a minute, pat yourself on the back, and jump back to 1.

People

Chapter 49: The Truth Will Set You Free

Do not lie.

It's a simple directive, but one that is very hard to carry out. In the corporate world and even in your private life, there are things you cannot share. People in work will frequently ask you questions that you are not allowed to answer, such as regarding financial data near the end of the year, or plans to downsize that are not yet public. You cannot always tell people everything, but be fair to them and tell them that the information is private or the timing would be harmful. They will understand or at least respect you for not just making up excuses.

Do not set up unreal expectations or give people false hope when you know the situation facing them is bad. Of course, you will feel under pressure when you have someone in front of you asking a direct question about a topic that will affect their livelihood. Trying to soften the eventual blow by saying things like "I will see what I can do," "it may not end this way," or "I will raise your issue with the boss" when you know you can't actually do anything about the situation might be well-intentioned, but it is just unkind and will backfire on you. Not only can you not change the situation, but you have given them a target for their hurt or anger when the bad news comes, especially if you are the one who will have to deliver it.

The same applies to the more mundane things in work. If there is a problem with a product delivery, tell the customer. Do not pretend or lie; it will come back to catch you. Mistakes happen; things go wrong. Face them and deal with them. Do not hide.

There are companies in which the culture is so bad that those in the positions of power have repeatedly shown that they cannot handle bad news. Responding with anger or annoyance to bad news is a form of bullying and, in companies in which this is the norm, the work life is rarely healthy. It's a symptom of a badly dysfunctional organization. There may be little you can do in such situations and you can only hope those perpetrating the culture will leave or come to their senses. Otherwise, you may be the one who has to leave in order to preserve your integrity, dignity, or maybe just your sense of perspective.

To me, it is very simply a case that working without lies and without hiding issues is a much less stressful work life, because the complications that are born from compounded lies or festering problems are avoided.

Chapter 50: Speed

These days the world is obsessed with speed: Speed of decisions, speed of replies, and speed of execution. I now sympathize with all those hamsters you see running on the wheels in pet stores. The world moves so fast that when "the competition is ahead of us" or "the competition is biting at our heels," we're instructed to "go faster; go faster, more speed NOW".

I learned a great lesson about speed not too long ago, which was that it may not be the fastest person who wins; it will probably be the most agile person. After years of thinking about it, I signed up for one-day racetrack event at a local speedway. Participating drivers used their own cars and had to adhere to a very strict code of conduct on the track. In return, they received some time with instructors, and then got to experience the thrill of serious speed in relative safety. My car was a big four-door sedan, but had lots and lots of horsepower, and a few more thrown in when you pressed that magic M button. The instructor drove the car while I rode shotgun for the first few laps, so that I could see what the car was capable of when someone a lot braver than I was in control. He was good and I could not believe that my car could go around the track that fast. When it was my turn to drive, I went whizzing around the track, unleashing all the ponies, having a blast. On all the straights, the massive power of the car meant I got up to huge speeds. Being heavy, the car needed to drop a lot of speed for the corners. It was brilliant fun.

However, again and again I would see a Miata in my rearview mirror eagerly trying to get past me. Yes, while the Miata could not catch me on the straights, it could corner much faster because it was lighter and more agile. So, I "let" him pass — and after three or four corners, I could no longer keep up with him. My top speed was much higher, but his lower speed and agility beat me in the end.

Of course, there are times when neither your speed nor your agility are appreciated. I'm sure every person who reads this book has received emails stating one or more of the following message: "I sent you an email this morning and I have seen nothing from you." "I left a voice mail yesterday and I have not heard back." "I texted you and nothing, what gives?"

It would be so tempting to say, "I'll tell you 'what gives.' I prioritized your request below everything else I decided I would do today. You are being ignored and I will get to you when the volumes of items I really need to tend to are all taken care of." So, go ahead and say it. Feel free to

212

share your priority list and let people know that you are in fact working to a plan, even if that plan does not put them first.

When the list of work you have queued starts to get to be too much, make a quick visit to your "happy place." Think back to your best vacation ever, or even just having a cold beer sitting in a deck chair on you back porch. Doesn't that sound nice? Then jump back to reality and knock something else off the list.

You must take some sanity time or you will lose however much sanity you have left. Slow down every now and then. Your work life is not unlike driving—when travelling at speed, any miscalculation will cause a big accident or could just burn you out, so force yourself to slow down and think through what you are about to do. When you have taken those few minutes or hours to plan, you will be able to get back to full speed and avoid mistakes and be less surprised by some of those hairpin turns that come out of nowhere.

Speed is not a bad thing and it can actually be exhilarating to be barreling down that hill with a wide-mouthed grin. You can go even faster if you know the route and took the precaution to test your brakes before you got started.

And just in case anyone is interested, my racing career was exhilarating, but rather brief. Sadly, in the second session of the day, the bloody engine on my car blew up—caught fire and everything. The net result of my big racing adventure was about 40 minutes of racing pleasure, the charred hulk of a burned-out car with a hole in the top of engine, and one good story. My racing career is on hold—for now.

213

People

Chapter 51: Marathons – Meetings Without End

Be on time to your meetings. Be on time ending your meetings. Better yet, end them early, if everything is done. There are few things more frustrating and annoying than waiting around for the last stragglers to appear before you can start, yet you have 10 people in the room twiddling their thumbs or checking Faceplant on their phones, wasting company time. When the stragglers include your boss or someone up the food chain, it is even worse because now you will have to repeat the items they missed by being tardy.

One of my principle rules for meetings is only invite those who are needed to provide input or to be informed about something. If someone has nothing to contribute to the meeting, do not invite them. You are wasting their time and the company's money. Send them an email update afterward, if necessary.

All meetings estimated to take more than one hour need to be reviewed and probably changed or scrapped. They are more than likely too long. If the topics are valid and need a meeting to discuss or present, split the meeting into a few different meetings. This will help keep people's attention and will give people time to complete the routine tasks they need to do.

We live and work in a world with many time zones. Sometimes, you may need to repeat meetings to accommodate all the team members. When you take the case of a companywide address and the audience is all around the world, then you need to set times when people can reasonably join. I know that means you, being so important, need to repeat yourself. Deal with it and just plan to repeat yourself, repeat yourself.

Determining which items need to be on the agenda is somewhat of an art form. Considering that so many meetings go off the rails and people leave them feeling as if they are only another hour closer to death without having achieved something worthwhile, you need to prepare to have a good meeting. There are a few things you can do to achieve this.

- Be brave and run your meeting the way you want to run it. Do not let someone else hijack it, even if he or she is the boss.
- Remind people of the time and use that to push things forward.
- Constrain the topics of conversation to the actual point of the meeting and derail the casual additions people make from time to time.

216

- If the meeting has covered the needed topics, then end it. Do not let it deteriorate into the casual conversations that spring up when there is a moment's silence.
- Keep notes and publish the decisions that were made during the meeting.
- Record the new actions that you all agreed on and assign an owner to each, then publish those, as well.

Meetings can be very useful, but keep them short and sharp, and remember that the point of meetings should be to decide things and then get down to executing the things that were decided.

People

Chapter 52: Do Not Panic

As would be expected from an engineer of a certain age who grew up in a certain era, one of my favorite books within a book is *Hitchhikers Guide to The Galaxy's Encyclopedia Galactic*. In this book, the Earth is originally described as "harmless" and then, in the updated edition, as "mostly harmless." Extrapolating that genius description to the real world, it could easily be argued that, while being mostly harmless, Earthlings only need a very few very harmful individuals to screw everything up.

The same goes for companies.

Getting back to the *Encyclopedia Galactic,* I should explain that it is aimed at beings who are thinking of traversing the galaxy and will inevitably come across some very hairy situations. The *Encyclopedia* has a very useful phrase embossed on its front: "Don't Panic". This is the

219

best advice I can give you, too. When things fall apart, stay calm and collected. You can't fix anything in an atmosphere in which nothing is under control.

Panic leads humans to react by flight or fight. My suggestions for when you find yourself in a panic-inducing situation are:

1) Try *not* panicking.
2) Do *not* fight or flee; instead, pause, think, and think again.
3) Take a breath and slow your heartbeat a little.
4) Look at all the available facts that you can find, and then construct a plan and take action.

In most cases, taking those few extra seconds or minutes will mean that you make a better choice.

Clearly, there are exceptions. In the event that Wile E. Coyote has cut the cord on the 10-ton weight and it is falling toward you at terminal velocity, I recommend that you *don't* pause; just *move*. No need to panic, though.

My point is that there is a time and a place for action, but never one for panic, especially when what's facing you is a business-related problem, rather than imminent death.

Finding solutions to problems is one of my favorite things to do, and experience has taught me that there is always a solution. The one you end up implementing may not be the exact one you wanted, but it will be something and it will most likely help the situation. I never would manufacture a situation just to be able to "solve" it—for one thing, I don't need the adrenaline junkies around — but, when things need solving, then I take on the challenge and get it done. So should you.

People

Chapter 53: Доверяй, Но Проверяй (Trust, But Verify)

On a daily basis, there are so many things going on in even the smallest business that it is really impossible for a single person to control or be fully aware of the actions of their teams. In reality, you cannot even control a small part without having to trust people.

But whom to trust, what to trust them with, and what to do when trust is broken are three questions every manager has to face. Experience has taught us that people are not perfect. They will make mistakes in judgment every now and then, and some people will be plain malicious and surprise us with their ingenuity for creating havoc.

When trust is lost in the business world, there is no easy way to get it back. Sometimes, it is impossible to regain lost trust.

That being said, in my opinion there is BIG trust and small trust. You can trust someone to pick up the documents from the printer on the morning of the meeting. If they do not do it and have no believable excuse, you lose trust in them and will think twice about relying on them for other small, but important, tasks. This is small trust. Some of it can be regained and eventually may even be restored. It is like dropping a cup and a chip is knocked off it — with patience, it can be repaired and be almost as good as new. If the cup is dropped many times and chips each time, the continual need for repairs becomes a burden and eventually you just throw it away and get another one.

Then there is BIG trust. When BIG trust is lost or is broken, it causes a lot of destruction. It cannot be repaired; the original structure is damaged beyond recognition. BIG trust in work is broken when the finance people steal. It is broken when the manager lies about the promotion you did not get and does not admit that it is because you were not right for the job or that they just do not like you and chose someone they did like. It is when someone purposely takes advantage of a customer or colleague out of greed or anger. As a manager, I have had to deal with all of these situations and more.

The most memorable instance was wrong on so many levels. One of our salespeople was moonlighting for a competitor while on our payroll. The company found out when an irate distributor called the corporate office, livid because he thought he was being tested by the salesman when he offered the distributor an option to buy our competitor's products instead of ours. It was news to us. Absorbing our own shock

224

(without panicking, by the way), we had to inform the customer that he wasn't being tested; the salesman had gone rogue. The salesman and a few other cohorts in the company were unceremoniously suspended and locked out of their offices as an investigation was launched. It wasn't pretty and the suspicion it generated trickled out in all directions. The company recovered, the individuals involved lost their jobs, and it took a very long time before those directly affected found it possible to trust in our company again.

When trust is broken by someone, it's rarely by mistake. People are not oblivious to their own deceit. "I didn't realize what I was doing" or "I never meant to cause trouble" are some of the explanations you may hear. These are inevitably lies and compound the trust issue. Translated, what they really mean is "I got caught red handed and now I'll throw myself on the mercy of the court." Well, you can throw yourself out the door as far as I'm concerned. People who behave destructively deserve the full consequences their actions bring to them.

A corollary to never breaking trust is never to renege on a promise you have made, unless the company will be in danger if you don't. It is crucial that if you ever do need to renege on that promise, you must explain yourself truthfully and make it clear why you needed to break the promise.

Do not ever compromise on trust. There is nothing to be gained and much to lose. The salary or wage you get paid requires that you do the right thing and be a trustworthy person. If people lie or show an obvious lack of regard for the truth, if they continuously break the small trust, or ever break the BIG trust, then they need to go.

In my experience, the vast majority of people rarely have small trust issues and an even smaller group have BIG trust issues. So, I trust people initially and am watchful of their actions, which will either reinforce my trust or not. If trust issues arise, I handle them as they happen. Thankfully, they don't happen often.

I take to heart the message in a Russian proverb made famous in America by a former United States president: Доверяй, но проверяй. Trust, but verify.

Chapter 54: Loyalty

I always hear a lot of chatter about employee loyalty and employer loyalty. I think the days of such things are long gone, at least in most workplaces. I also do not think that is necessarily bad. This new reality doesn't mean the company will always try to take advantage of the employee or that the employee will try to deceive or cheat the company.

In the past, what was called 'loyalty' was, in fact, a characteristic mistakenly attributed to the worker-company relationship. The business environment as it was up until the second half of the 20th century was not as competitive as it is today and the speed at which competitors could enter the market was much slower. This environment allowed companies to meander along doing the same old thing, happy to ensure the status quo in part by keeping the workers happy. The longer-term employment resulting from this was misinterpreted as company loyalty

227

and as employee loyalty. The environment is different now, and so should be the language we use to describe it. It's not as catchy, but replace the loyalty premise with just behaving yourself and being a good corporate citizen while in return expecting to receive fair treatment and compensation for doing a job well and accepting that everything is driven by the profit motive and 'adjustments' will need to be made to keep the money flowing.

Chapter 55: What Now?

Getting organized and staying organized is a challenge that most people can overcome, but not all, for some bizarre reason.

In reality, the secret to becoming organized is simple:

Step 1: Take up to 30 minutes to think about all the things you need to get done in the next few days and weeks.

Step 2: Take up to 10 minutes to make a list of all the things you thought of in Step 1.

Step 3: Take up to five minutes for each item listed in Step 2 to determine its completion date. Write it down.

Step 4: Take up to four minutes for each item listed in Step 2 to determine who needs to do it. Write it down.

Step 5: Share the list with the people whose names you have put on it and get their buy-in.

Step 6: Collectively, start working through the list. Add new things as they come up and delete completed things.

Step 7: Work happily ever after; rinse and repeat.

It really IS that simple. However, getting up the will to do it is your own problem to solve, and helping you with that is beyond my pay grade.

Chapter 56: Problem Solving

Solutions: One always exists. As a manager, your job is to find it.

It is astounding that there appears to be a significant lack of problem-solving skills out there. You come across people who appear to be incapable of action in the face of a problem, or those who come up with unbelievable and useless solutions. I wonder sometimes if the ability to solve problems is instinctive or if it can be taught and learned.

To me, problem solving is usually, not always, very simple and solutions are plain to see, and I'm never certain why people get so worked up when confronted by a problem. To be blunt, I think people like playing the hero and the martyr. They think that if a problem can be solved without drama, then it will make them seem not very clever. As in, if discussing the problem involves high levels of consternation and gnashing of teeth, then the person who solves it must be valuable.

231

Here's a little quiz. Your customers are complaining that you are not shipping them parts on time. Which of the following solutions seems or feels right to you, and which would be the preferred solution for different members of your team?

A. Replace the whole ordering system.

B. Change every process and document all your failings.

C. Be more organized and record when orders come in and are shipped, and for those orders that take too long to deliver, do something.

D. Blame your coworkers, but don't do anything more.

E. Blame your manager's decision to reduce inventory two years ago, but don't do anything more.

F. Blame everyone, but don't do anything more.

G. Do something.

If your answer was anything other than C or G, you are likely part of the problem.

Here is a brief approach to problem solving. These steps are at the heart of all good methods:

- Reproduce the issue.
- Change something.
- Determine if the problem is still happening.
- If not, it is probably fixed.
- If it is, go back to the top of this list and start over.
- Determine if too much time has passed without having solved the problem.
- If not, then keep going.
- If it has, then get more help – NOW!!

Part VII – The Point

People

Chapter 57: Smell the Roses

If you let one reason to celebrate pass without a celebration, then you have just wasted many staff years of effort. If you honestly do not care to celebrate things, then don't—but you need to get a different job working with non-humans. Try skunks or bits of rock.

In other words, be a decent human and remember to celebrate the successes you achieve.

If you are one of those people who doesn't like to have fun, please recognize that most other people seem to be receptive to having some fun, so put on your big boy or big girl underpants and throw a bloody party, or at least order in pizza for lunch. If you just can't help making it unapologetically clear to everyone just how much of a miserable bastard you are, then, please, rethink working with those skunks or stones. Everyone will be glad to see you go.

If you are someone who enjoys a good celebration, then pick an achievement for the year and try to make it the group goal. When you look back on the year, there will be something tangible to celebrate. I have work and personal achievements; my latest is to learn to play the piano and, not just that, but to play a particular song. When I achieve that, you can believe I'll throw a party to show off.

People appreciate the pause that celebration brings and the punctuation that is naturally needed between the end of one useful effort and the beginning of the next one. It gives everyone much-needed time to think about what was achieved and to think about what it is they are about.

If what your group has achieved doesn't warrant a celebration, at least make sure to give praise publicly. But only do so for things that are complete; you don't want to let your people think they'll be rewarded for potentially wasted effort that may or may not result in some good.

There are some special cases that you should celebrate even though the outcome was not what was wanted. I learned this recently following a very harrowing bid that required tens of people to perform under pressure for more than six months. Being successful in the customer bid would increase the company profits significantly, so the team was given the instruction to go all out. They really did not need to be told that. They had been around long enough to understand the importance of winning the bid; there had never been a more self-motivated team put together in the company. Night and day, weekends and holidays, the preparation and tests continued, the bid was completed and the trial was launched.

Nearly four months later, the customer made their choice. Unfortunately, the team effort had not won the day. The customer was very complimentary and told us it was a very close competition but, in the end, we were just not selected. We celebrated anyway. Not the win, obviously, but we wanted to acknowledge the effort put in by the team publicly thank them for all the hard work that they did.

My advice to celebrate more than just the wins circles back to a point that I've made elsewhere in this book: Do not make the mistake of valuing money or achievement above life. Having too narrow a focus is an obvious and ridiculous mistake. Your life will not be fuller because the widget has one new function that no one else thought of. It will be fuller because you stopped to enjoy what you achieved.

To torture yet another cliché, remember to stop and smell the roses — even the little scrubby ones that you'd never pick for your sweetheart still smell lovely.

People

Chapter 58: The Good

Life can be sweet; work can be sweet. You get to meet lots of people, most of whom are not assholes.

Every now and then, you see a smile as a reaction to something you do.

Every now and then, you learn a very interesting piece of knowledge.

Every now and then, you have nothing to do and peace descends.

Every now and then, you manage to achieve something special and it makes you feel very good.

People

Chapter 59: Home Life

This is a book about how to recognize, think about, and hopefully deal with some of the many situations you will find yourself experiencing during the normal course of work. However, there is such a thing as life outside of work and you need to try to be happy there, as well. There is no real division between a work life and a home life; what happens in one impacts the other, stresses in one affect the other, successes in one will have positive effects on the other.

Most of us need to work. Some work for sanity reasons, but most of us work at least for the money, so we can use it for the things we need or want. Be that as it may, it is important to keep things in perspective and remember your home life.

Work will put pressure on you — sometimes extreme pressure — and there will be times that you will feel as if work is all there is.

Unfortunately, you may find yourself with a bad boss who actually enjoys it when you are worried about your job. Sometimes, there is an expectation that the "company" deserves your unwavering loyalty and that you should dedicate all your waking time to delivering whatever it is the company profits from. Even in such lopsided situations, I urge you to try hard to divide work from the central meaning of your life, your home life. It will translate to a healthier life inside of work.

Epilogue

According to the dictionary on the Interwebs—yes, sometimes I'm that lazy—an epilogue is 'a short chapter or section at the end of a literary work, sometimes detailing the fate of its characters.'

Well, this epilogue is short, so it meets Criterion Number One. It may also detail the fate of its characters, or at least its main character, which is you, the reader.

When I set out to write this book, I wanted it to be a self-realization book more than just a standard 'business book.' Here is what I hope you will take away from this book:

I want you to find a way to be happy and live a happy life. It will certainly be a great mixture of ups and downs, and will include a great mixture of characters you meet who may depend on you and on whom your very career or happiness will seem to hinge. Embrace it.

Understand that life is not simple and there is no simple answer to many questions, so do not look for them. Accept it.

Feel free to reach for the stars, but do not spend all your energy looking for a utopia in your personal or professional life. You'll be disappointed because it's not there to be found and you cannot create one. Instead, set your sights on what is plainly around you and within your grasp and what makes you happy. Don't keep moving your goal posts because of external pressures or the flavor of the day. Being mundane and grounded can be brilliant and can bring great happiness. The place you are happiest should be your 'happy place.' Enjoy it.

Good luck. And don't forget to have some fun.

About the author

I have spent nearly 30 years in the business world listening and learning, beginning with my first paying job as a 14-year-old in Dublin, Ireland teaching basic computer skills to adults, through summer jobs in high school working on building sites in London digging ditches, doing carpentry, laying bricks, and driving construction vehicles around building sites.

While earning my engineering degree, my first professional job was programming software in a disk duplication factory as a summer intern in Hyannis, Massachusetts. Between then and now, I have worked all over the world as a software developer and architect, project and program manager, vice president of engineering and chief technology officer, general manager and company president, founder of a startup, and author.

I'm not finished by a long shot, but it has become very apparent to me over the course of my career that I have a somewhat unique take on the business world and an individual's — every individual's — place or role in it.

Made in the USA
Columbia, SC
28 January 2018